FOOTPATHS FOR FITNESS

AROUND BRISTOL & BATH

Nigel Vile

COUNTRYSIDE BOOKS
NEWBURY BERKSHIRE

First published 2009

COUNTRYSIDE BOOKS
3 Catherine Road
Newbury, Berkshire

To view our complete range of books,
please visit us at
www.countrysidebooks.co.uk

ISBN: 978 1 84674 134 0

Photographs and maps by the author

Designed by Peter Davies, Nautilus Design
Produced through MRM Associates Ltd., Reading
Typeset by CJWT Solutions, St Helens
Printed in Thailand

CONTENTS

GRADE 1 – STROLL

GRADE 2 – STRIDE

FOOTPATHS FOR FITNESS

FOOTPATHS FOR FITNESS

GRADE 3 – HIKE

Introduction

The benefits of regular exercise are frequently extolled in the press and in doctors' surgeries, and yet statistics show that few of us heed this advice. Two in three men, for example, and three in four women do less than 30 minutes moderate intensity activity on at least five days a week. Of course we have our excuses! It may be lack of time due to work or family commitments, it could be the cost of equipment or gym membership or there may be a lack of facilities nearby. There are also safety issues – concerns about exercising outdoors alone or poor weather or lack of night-time lighting. None of these issues should throw up barriers to exercising, however, because there are many simple steps that could help. It could be walking up stairs rather than using lifts, or even doing the housework at double time!

Studies have shown that regular exercise can have a number of significant benefits. These include:

- reducing the risk of coronary heart disease and stroke
- lowering blood pressure
- reducing high cholesterol and improving blood lipid profile
- reducing body fat
- enhancing mental well being
- increasing bone density, hence helping to prevent osteoporosis
- reducing the risk of cancer of the colon
- reducing the risk of non insulin dependent diabetes
- helping to control body weight
- helping remedy osteoarthritis
- helping flexibility and co-ordination hence reducing the risk of falls

(Sources: Davison & Grant 1993, US Department of Health 1996, British Heart Foundation 2000)

Walking provides one of the best forms of exercise, and counters all of those arguments put forward for not taking regular exercise. If time is an issue, then simply get off the bus a stop earlier and walk for 10 minutes or park the car at the far end of the supermarket car-park and take a brief stroll. As for expense – walking as a form of exercise is almost free. All that is required are some old clothes, stout shoes and a waterproof coat – probably the sort of things that you would wear gardening. Of course, the outdoor pursuit shops are full of expensive and heavily branded items of clothing and equipment, but most of these are unnecessary. Look at old photographs of

W.A. Poucher or Alfred Wainwright, and they look suitably dressed for a morning at the allotment rather than a day in the hills. Very little equipment is needed – maybe a rucksack to carry a drink and a snack, a map and a camera – but very little else. Walking does not require membership of a club or society, it can be undertaken 365 days of the year, it does not require a particular level of skill or expertise and it can be incorporated into a host of everyday activities such as shopping or travelling to work.

This book is an attempt to introduce the delights of walking to anybody resident in or visiting the Bath and Bristol area. It is designed to add an extra dimension to walking, taking the reader out into the great outdoors rather than simply walking to the local shop or up a flight of stairs. With this in mind the walks are graded, starting with a gentle stroll of just 1 mile, with no real gradients or stiles along the way, right through to a lengthy route of 7 miles, with a good steep climb and a sprinkling of stiles. In between are walks that make ever-increasing demands, with hills and stiles slowly being introduced in order to present slight challenges and a growing sense of achievement. As a rule of thumb, you can expect to burn off 100 calories for every mile walked, but this will vary with the nature of the terrain and the temperature during the day. This may seem a fairly inconsequential number of calories to lose, but this is on top of those calories expended in the everyday business of work and domestic activity – so it all helps! There is a suggested refreshment facility on each route – which might counter the calorie loss argument – but even the most unhealthy of pub menus will include salads or sandwiches, whilst fruit juices and mineral water sit alongside the beer taps and whisky dispensers.

If you work your way through these walks, not only will there be the health benefit – there will also be the opportunity to explore some of the fine countryside in the Bath and Bristol area. It may be the southern Cotswolds with villages such as Ford or Castle Combe, it could be the Avon Valley, near Keynsham and Hanham, for example, or even the vast expanses of the Severn estuary at Severn Beach and Littleton-on-Severn. There are walks on the top of open hills such as at Lansdown and Marshfield, or in sheltered river valleys in places like Hambrook and Monkton Combe.

Each walk comes with a good deal of practical information including:

- an outline of the walk's attractions
- the length of each route
- the terrain along the way
- the estimated number of calories that will be expended on the walk
- the relevant Ordnance Survey map
- how to get to the start of each walk

- parking arrangements and possible public transport links to the walk
- walk directions that tie in with a sketch map
- a suggested refreshment break

The walks have a 6-figure grid reference for the starting point – a number such as 342674 – that might appear confusing to many readers. Think of it as that game called 'battleships'. In the game, there would be a grid with letters along the bottom and numbers up the side. C4 would mean 3 squares across and 4 squares up. Ordnance Survey maps work on the same principle, with each sheet being divided up into squares and a number appearing on each line that makes up these squares. That number quoted earlier would simply mean that you go along to line number 34 and then across two-tenths of the next square, before going up to line 67 and on another four tenths into the next square. If you have trouble remembering whether it is along the bottom or up the side first, remember what you do when entering a house – in through the door – that is along the bottom – and then up the stairs. Enough of this technical map-reading exercise – if you are at all confused, simply read the directions on how to get to the start of each walk and I am sure there will be no problem.

In conclusion, I hope that you receive a whole host of benefits from these walks. There is the opportunity to explore the fine natural landscape near Bath and Bristol, as well as to spend time relaxing with friends and family. There is also the chance to realise that regular exercise need not be a daunting and expensive activity, and that such activity can lead to a whole range of health benefits. I trust that you will enjoy walking each of these routes as much as I did, and that you will be even more appreciative of what a lovely part of the country we are fortunate enough to live in.

Nigel Vile

Publisher's Note

We hope that you obtain considerable enjoyment from this book; great care has been taken in its preparation. Although at the time of publication all routes followed public rights of way or permitted paths, diversion orders can be made and permissions withdrawn.

We cannot, of course, be held responsible for such diversion orders and any inaccuracies in the text which result from these or any other changes to the routes nor any damage which might result from walkers trespassing on private property. We are anxious though that all details covering the walks are kept up to date and would therefore welcome information from readers which would be relevant to future editions.

The simple sketch maps that accompany the walks in this book are based on notes made by the author whilst checking out the routes on the ground. They are designed to show you how to reach the start, to point out the main features of the overall circuit and they contain a progression of numbers that relate to the paragraphs of the text.

However, for the benefit of a proper map, we do recommend that you purchase the relevant Ordnance Survey sheet covering your walk. The Ordnance Survey maps are widely available, especially through booksellers and local newsagents

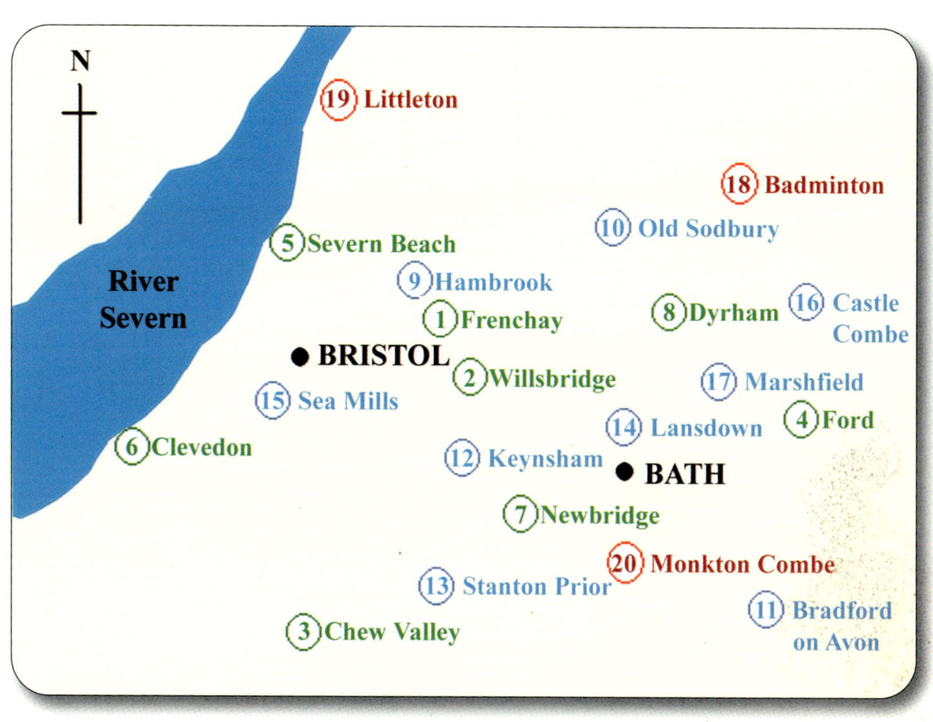

Area map showing location of the walks

Grade 1 – STROLL

Grade 2 – STRIDE

Grade 3 – HIKE

1 Oldbury Court and the River Frome

FOOTPATHS FOR FITNESS

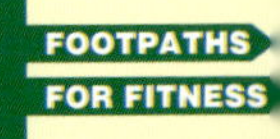

By Riverside and Woodland

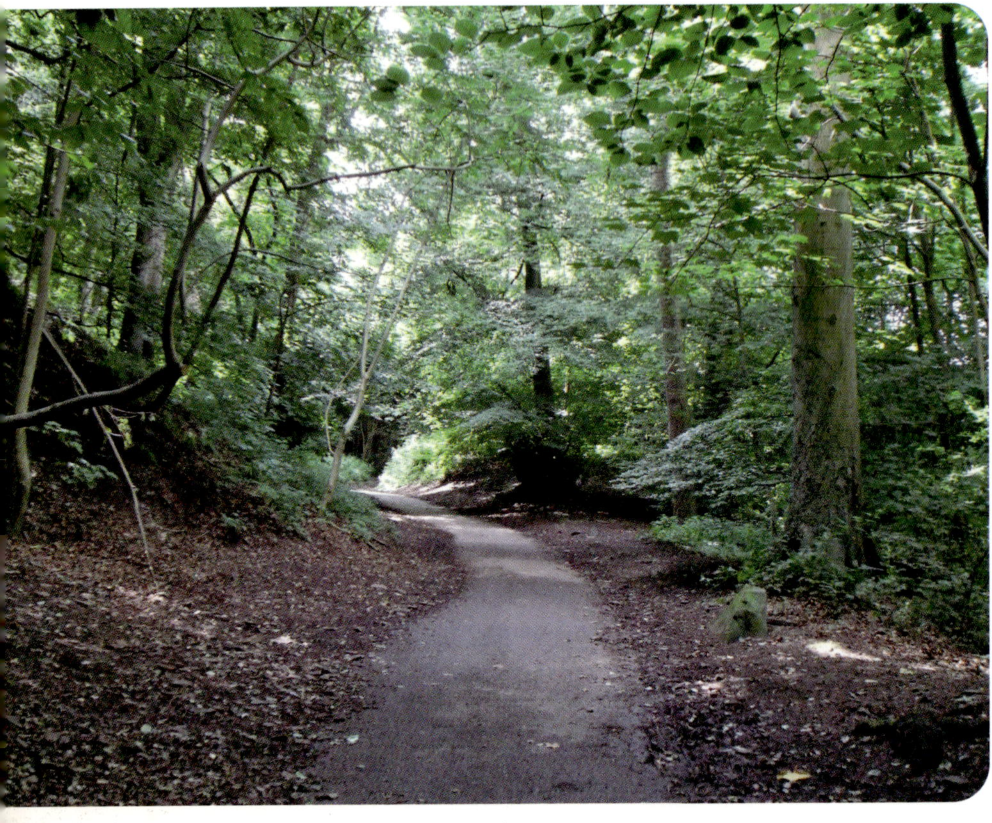

■ *An inviting woodland path* ■

Oldbury Court may no longer have its estate house but the stunning woodland, historic parkland and riverside paths all combine to create a backdrop for some delightful walking. Flowing through a steep-sided and often rocky valley is the river Frome, less than 5 miles from its confluence with the Avon in the heart of Bristol. The tree cover is majestic, and makes this a particularly exhilarating autumnal excursion when the red and orange, yellow and brown foliage form a dramatic backdrop. This is the first walk on your way to fitness and, despite being low on miles, is never short of interest and intrigue.

■ *The river Frome with its majestic tree cover* ■

GRADE: 1
ESTIMATED CALORIE BURN: 100

Distance: 1 mile
Stiles: None
Terrain: With just the occasional gentle climb along the way, this is a very straightforward walk. A short section of the riverside path can be muddy underfoot following heavy rainfall.
Time: 1 hour
Map: OS Explorer 155
Starting point: GR 640772
Directions to Start / Parking / Public Transport: Follow the B4058 Bristol to Wotton-under-Edge road to the main entrance to Frenchay Hospital. Turn into Begbrook Park at this point, and follow the road around towards Frenchay Common. In 300 yards, turn right and follow Pearce's Hill downhill to a bridge over the river Frome. Park on the roadside just by the bridge. *First* run a regular daily bus service from the centre of Bristol to Frenchay.
Refreshments: At the end of the walk, drive back up to Frenchay Common and take the first turning on the right. This will bring you to the White Lion Inn which offers a wide range of non-alcoholic beverages, as well as salads, sandwiches and vegetarian options.

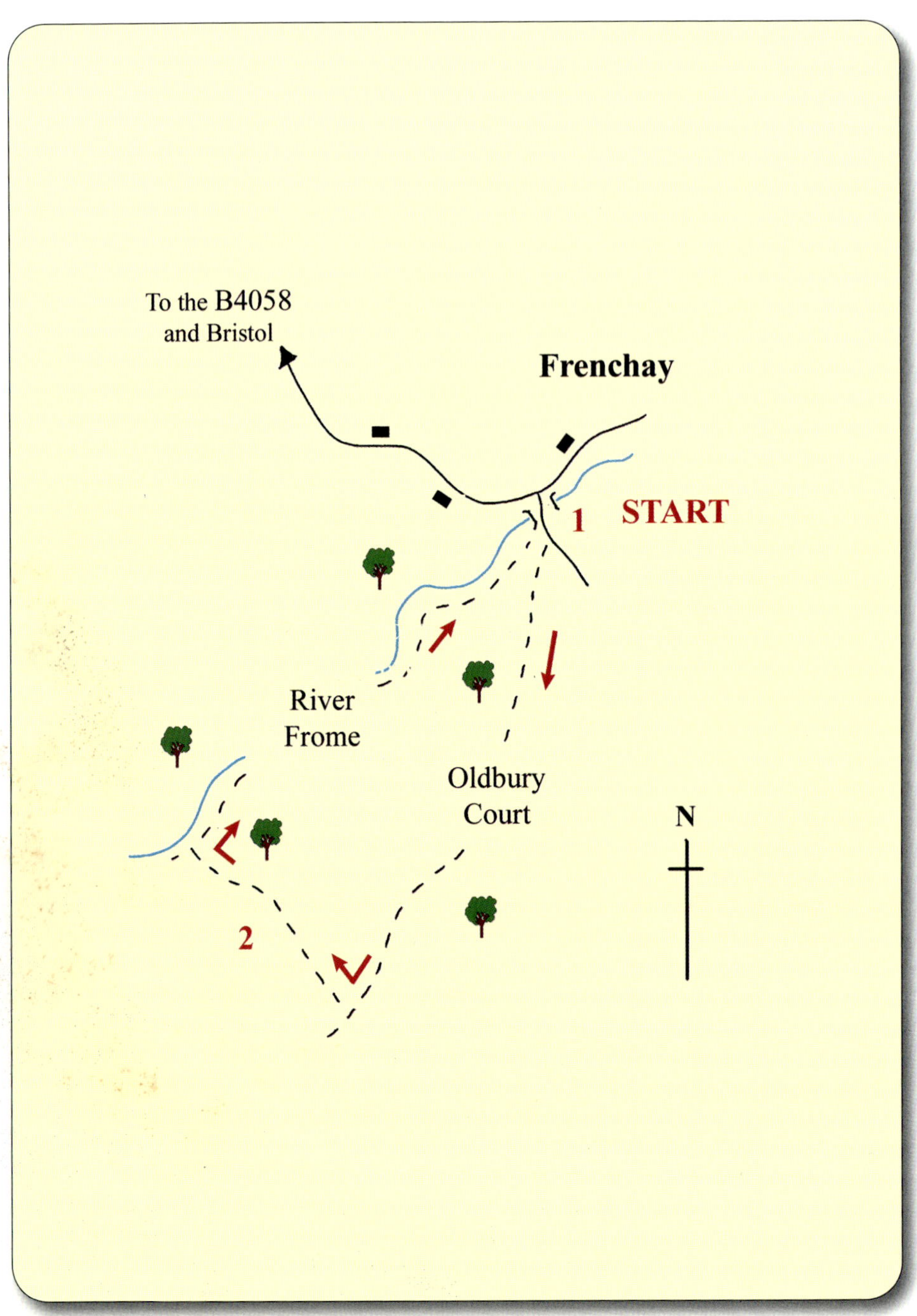
To the B4058
and Bristol
Frenchay
1
START
River
Frome
Oldbury
Court
N
2

■ *The river runs within a steep-sided valley* ■

1 Cross the bridge and turn right into **Oldbury Court**. In a few yards, at a fork, follow the main tarmac path ahead – not the path on the right that drops down to the **river Frome**. Follow the path uphill through the trees for 200 yards before continuing across an area of open grassland for 300 yards. Just before the path drops downhill to cross a stream, turn right and follow a path downhill with the stream on the left.

2 After 150 yards, at a junction, follow a path to the left that drops downhill to the **river Frome** in the valley bottom with the tributary stream on the left all the while. Follow the Frome to the right for 600 yards to a point where the path climbs some steps to reach the road and bridge crossed at the outset. Turn left, and cross the river to return to your vehicle.

2 The Willsbridge Valley

A Hidden Oasis of Calm

■ *A wetland habitat* ■

Willsbridge, on the eastern fringes of Bristol, is not obvious walking country. Hidden away amongst the sprawling estates and main roads, however, is the Willsbridge valley, dissected by the Siston Brook, a veritable oasis of calm in the midst of 21st-century hustle and bustle. The wooded valley is home to bats and owls, squirrels and foxes, jays and badgers, whilst the river provides a perfect habitat for the kingfisher and the dipper. Alongside Willsbridge Mill, now an Avon Wildlife Trust Education Centre, is a series of ponds that are home to water boatmen and dragonflies. With its emphasis on rich and varied flora and fauna, this is very much a walk on the wild side.

1 Cross **Long Beach Road** and follow the path opposite and slightly to the right, downhill into the woodland bordering the **Willsbridge Mill Reserve**. In 200 yards, at a junction, turn left and follow a path through the valley, with **Siston Brook** below on the right, for 300 yards to a junction. Pass through the gateway opposite, and continue following the path ahead through the valley for 300 yards to a gateway and back lane. A detour uphill to the left will bring you to **Oldland church**.

■ *The fast-flowing Siston Brook is home to kingfishers* ■

2 *For the main walk*, cross a footbridge on the right to reach a small housing estate. Follow the cul de sac to the right for 150 yards and, where the road

GRADE: 1
ESTIMATED CALORIE BURN: 125

Distance: 1¼ miles
Stiles: None
Terrain: Level and well-defined paths run through the Willsbridge Valley. There is just one gentle descent into the valley from the car park, and an easy climb back again at journey's end.
Time: 1¼ hours
Map: OS Explorer 155
Starting point: GR 663711
Directions to Start / Parking / Public Transport: Leave the A431 at the top of Willsbridge Hill 1 mile south-east of Hanham and turn into Long Beach Road. After 350 yards, park in the Willsbridge Mill car park on the left-hand side of the road. *First* run a regular daily bus service from the centre of Bristol to Willsbridge.
Refreshments: At the end of the walk, return to the A431 and turn left towards Bath. In just over ½ mile, you will reach the headquarters of the Avon Valley Railway at Bitton. At the station is an excellent café and tea shop.

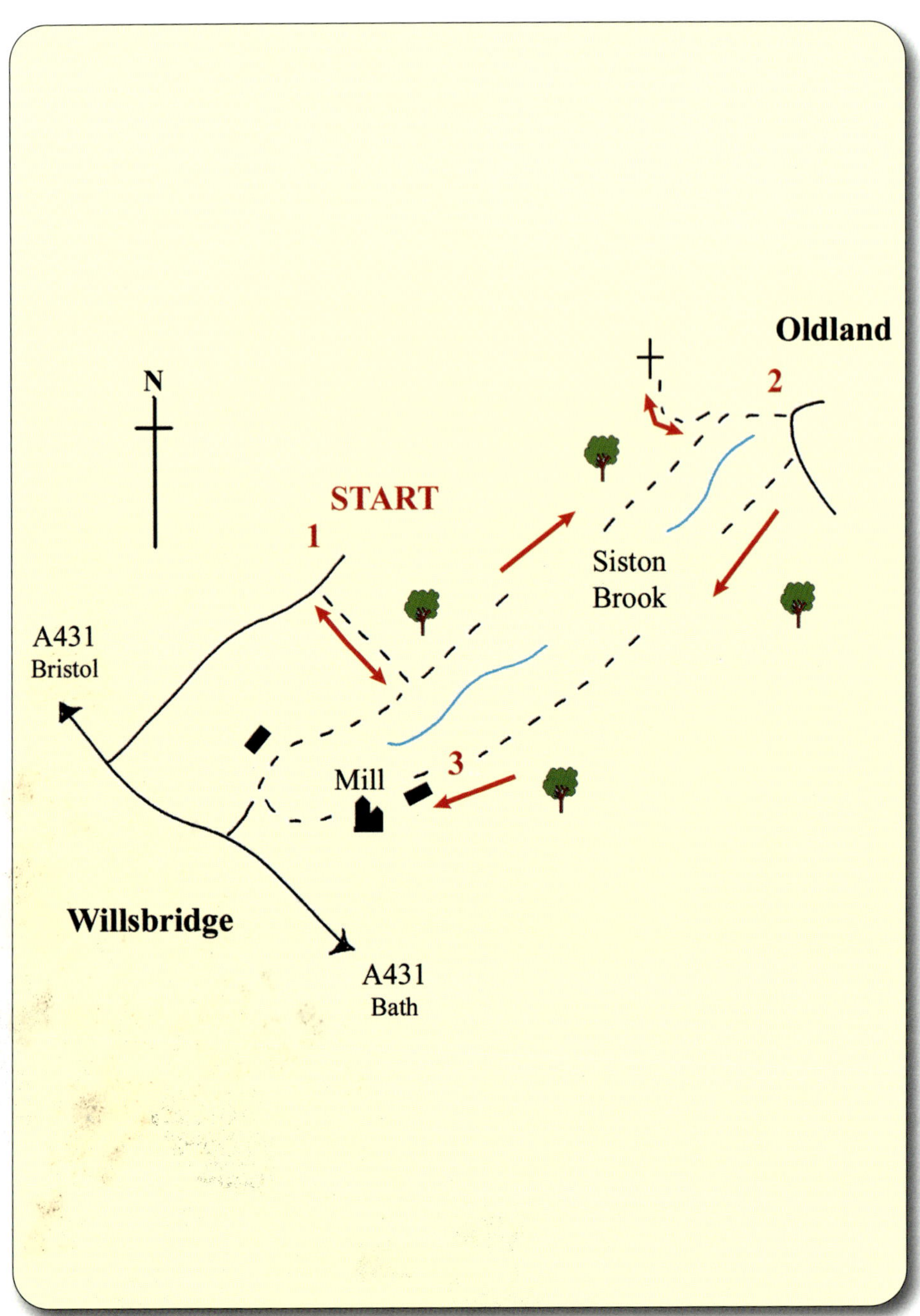
Oldland
N
2
START
1
Siston
Brook
A431
Bristol
Mill
3
Willsbridge
A431
Bath

■ *Willsbridge Mill, now the education centre of the Avon Wildlife Trust* ■

is blocked by some bollards, continue ahead for a few yards to a hand gate on the right. Follow a footpath down to a stile, turn sharp left and follow a path above **Siston Brook** – now below in the valley on the right. In 150 yards, ignore a path going off to the right and continue on the main path through the valley. In 300 yards, cross a stile and drop downhill towards **Willsbridge Mill**.

3 Just before a whitewashed cottage, turn right along to a pond. Follow the path to the left of the pond to reach a path on the right leading down to **Siston Brook**. Just beyond this path, follow a stepped path on the left that drops down to reach the mill and adjoining education centre. Follow the path ahead to a junction, bear right along a lane and continue to a junction in front of some properties. Turn right, and follow the path ahead through the valley above **Siston Brook** for 200 yards to a junction. Turn left, and retrace your steps back uphill to **Long Beach Road** and the car park.

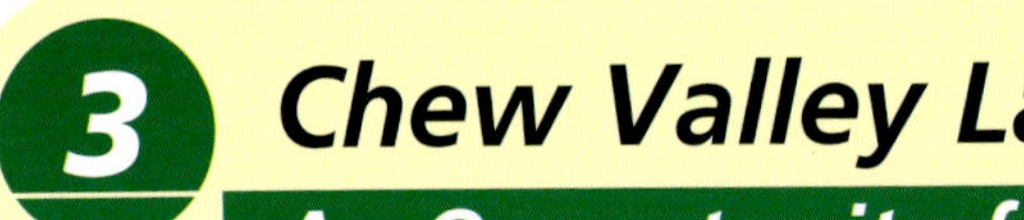

3 Chew Valley Lake

An Opportunity for Birdwatching

■ *Chew Lake* ■

Every major city demands vast quantities of water – and Bristol is no exception. Chew Valley Lake, 2½ miles long and with a capacity of some 4,500 million gallons, supplies much of the city's needs. Work on the reservoir commenced in 1950, with the Queen performing the official opening ceremony in 1956. As well as a water supply, the reservoir is an important leisure amenity. Fishermen travel considerable distances to fish for brown and rainbow trout, whilst for ornithologists it is an important centre for winter wildfowl, with diving birds such as the pochard and the tufted duck being especially common. This walk includes parts of two nature trails – the Grebe Trail and the Bittern Trail – with extensive reedbeds and woodland along the way, as well as the opportunity to take in a spot of birdwatching, either from the lakeside paths or from a secluded hide.

1 Just past a wooden hut at the entrance to the car park, turn left along a gravelled path. Follow this path for ¼ mile through to the next picnic area and car park, **Chew Lake** on the right all the while. At the far side of the car park is the start of the **Grebe Trail**. At an initial fork, follow the gravelled path to the left across grassland and scrub. Continue through some woodland and on across open ground, keeping on the path as it bears right and walk as far as a junction by some small ponds. Turn left, cross a bridge over **Hollow Brook** and follow a path to the right down through some staggered wooden fencing to an old streambed. Cross this streambed and follow the **Bittern Trail** to the right.

2 Follow this path – it soon bears left – and almost immediately right, along to a footbridge and raised causeway. A detour to the right just before this bridge will bring you to a hide. *For the main walk*, follow the raised causeway until it ends at a junction. Turn left, and follow a path along the rear of some woodland – open fields to the right – to a junction passed

GRADE: 1
ESTIMATED CALORIE BURN: 125

Distance: 1¾ miles
Stiles: None
Terrain: Level paths alongside Chew Valley Lake. Following rainfall, the paths around the hide on the Bittern Trail can become muddy.
Time: 1 hour
Map: OS Explorer 155
Starting point: GR 574614
Directions to Start / Parking / Public Transport: Follow the A368 – which links Bath and Weston-super-Mare, to the village of Bishop Sutton. At the eastern end of the village, turn onto the unclassified road that is signposted to Chew Valley Lake. In just over 1 mile, this road passes a picnic area on the left. Continue along the road for another ½ mile before turning left to park at the next picnic area. Chew Valley Lake is not served by regular public transport.
Refreshments: The Chew Valley Lake teashop is located alongside the car park.

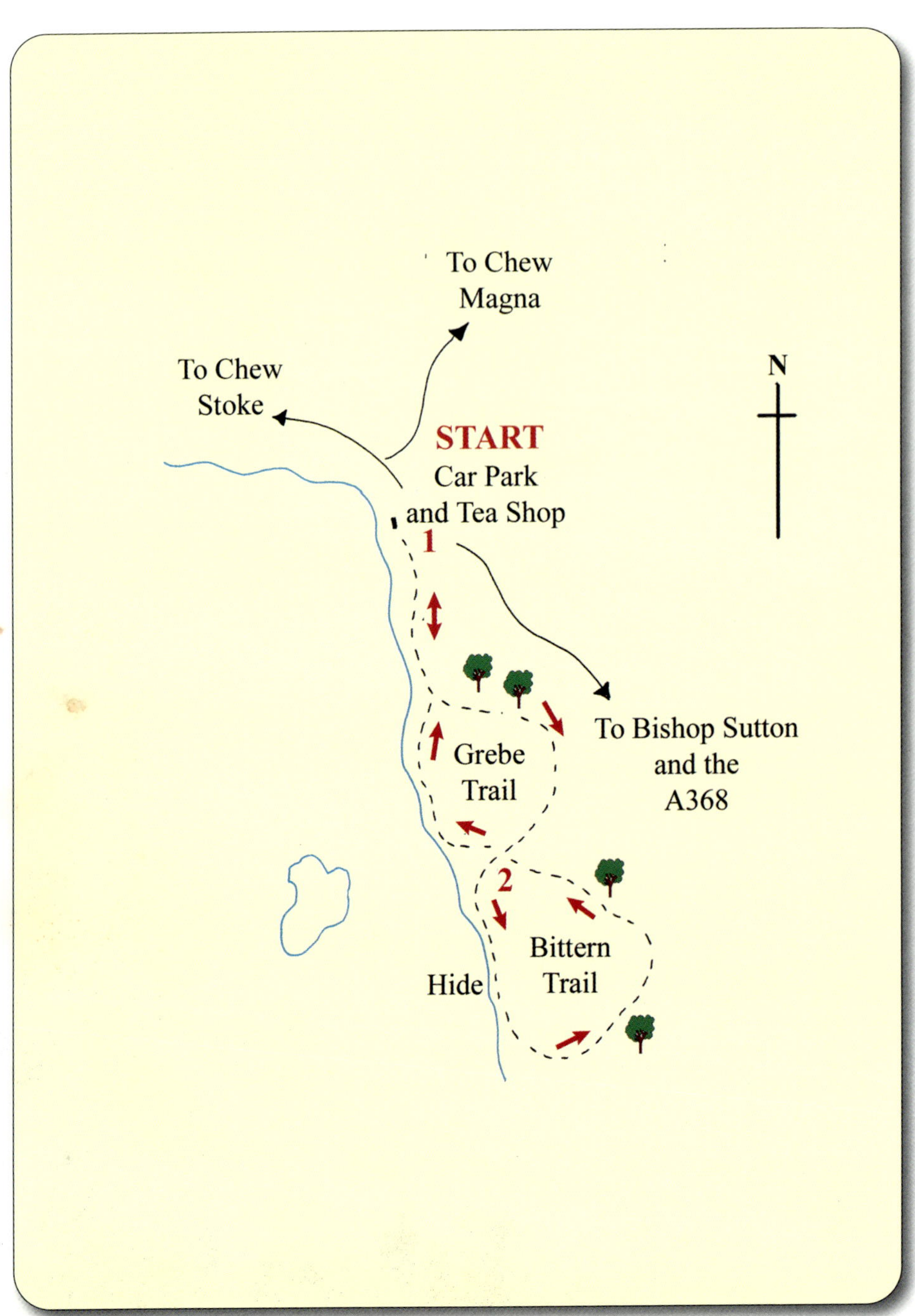
To Chew
Magna
To Chew
Stoke
N
START
Car Park
and Tea Shop
1
Grebe
Trail
To Bishop Sutton
and the
A368
2
Bittern
Trail
Hide

■ *The bridge over Hollow Brook* ■

earlier. Turn right, cross the old streambed and turn right up to the staggered fencing. Follow the path back up to the bridge over **Hollow Brook** to reach a junction with the **Grebe Trail**. Take the left-hand fork, and follow the gravelled path back along to the car park and picnic area. Walk through the car park and retrace your steps along the gravelled path alongside **Chew Lake** back to the initial car park.

4 Slaughterford and the By Brook Valley

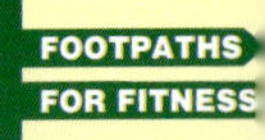

Far from the Madding Crowd

■ *The delightful By Brook* ■

The estate agent's adage 'location location location' certainly rings true in the case of Slaughterford, a diminutive hamlet deep in the By Brook Valley. Being in the heart of the southern Cotswolds, every building is of stone – the golden limestone for which the region is so famous – an isolated church, a scattering of farms, a few cottages and the occasional rather grand house, and little more. With a main road in neither sight nor sound, Slaughterford is truly far from the madding crowd. The By Brook itself is arguably the most beautiful of the Bristol Avon's tributary streams.

Its clear waters are home to a good number of trout, with the fishing rights being jealously guarded, whilst the surrounding meadows and wooded hillsides provide a range of habitats for several species of wildfowl.

■ *An interested inhabitant of a farm in Slaughterford* ■

1 Walk to the Bristol end of the lay-by and turn left down a stepped path to emerge by the **White Hart Inn** in **Ford**. Cross over and follow the lane opposite that runs alongside the inn. Cross the **By Brook** and, in 30 yards, turn right along a quiet side lane. Follow this lane for 600 yards as it climbs through **Common Hill**

GRADE: 1
ESTIMATED CALORIE BURN: 175

Distance: 1¾ miles
Stiles: 3
Terrain: This is the first walk that will begin to test your leg and lung power. Although the By Brook Valley offers easy riverside walking, there is one short but sharp climb out of Ford through Common Hill Plantation. The lane is marked with a pair of black arrows on the OS map, indicating a gradient of 20 per cent.
Time: 1½ hours
Map: OS Explorer 156
Starting point: GR 841749
Directions to Start / Parking / Public Transport: Initially make for the Cold Ashton roundabout, 5 miles east of Bristol on the A420 to Chippenham and 5 miles north of Bath on the A46 to Stroud. Continue along the A420 towards Chippenham for 6 miles to Ford where, alongside the main road opposite the church, is a small lay-by. Ford is not served by regular public transport.
Refreshments: The White Hart at Ford enjoys a delightful location near the By Brook.

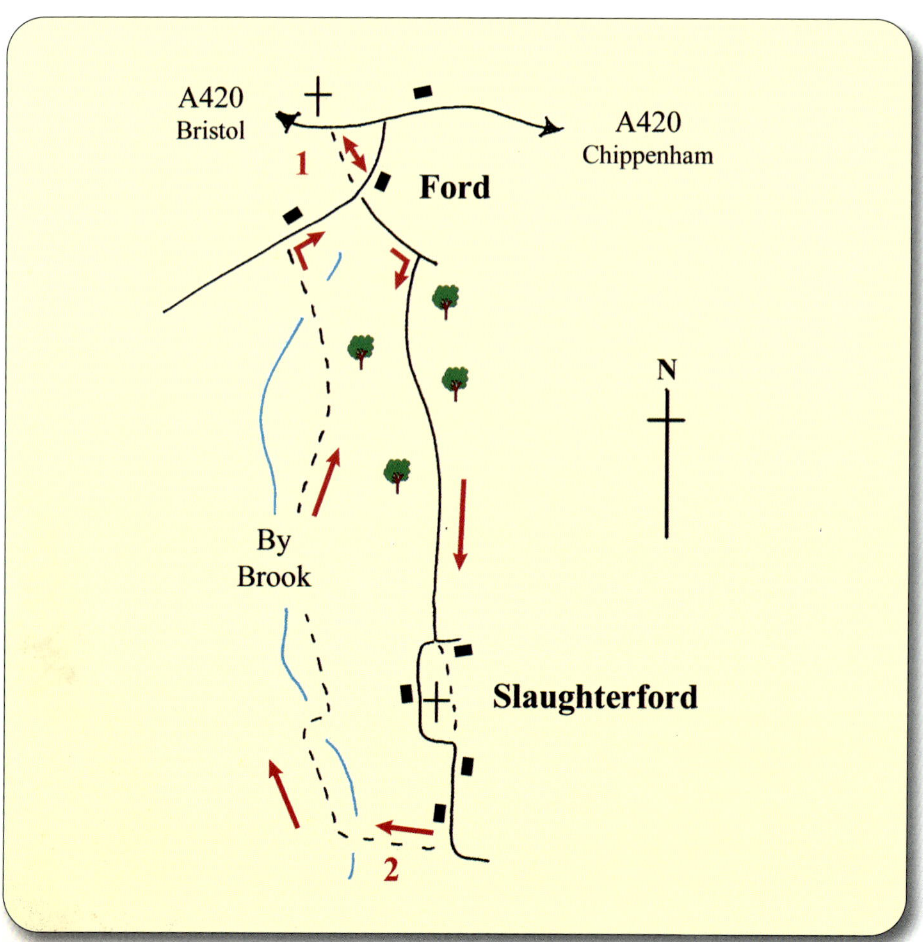

Plantation, before dropping down to a junction on the edge of **Slaughterford**. Cross the stile opposite into a field containing Slaughterford church. Cross this field, passing to the left of the church, to a gate in the opposite field boundary. Follow the raised pavement ahead through **Slaughterford** and, where the road bears left, turn right through a gateway and follow a footpath through woodland down to footbridges over the **By Brook**.

2 Cross these bridges and follow the river ahead upstream to a footbridge and sluices. Turn right, cross the river and turn left to follow the **By Brook** upstream. Aim for a stile in the far right corner of the first riverside meadow,

■ *Slaughterford church* ■

before making for the next stile on the far side of the second meadow, the By Brook still flowing along on the left. In the following field, aim for a footbridge and sluices in the far right corner before following the river upstream for 75 yards. Just past the second of two seats on the riverbank, bear left away from the river to a gate in the corner of the field. Join the Colerne to Ford road, turn right and continue for 200 yards to the **White Hart**. The road can be relatively busy so be careful. Turn left opposite the inn back up the stepped path to the A420 and the lay-by.

Severn Beach and the Severn Estuary

A Riverside Promenade

The Second Severn Crossing, completed in 1996

There is something rather magical about river estuaries, where fresh water meets the sea and where, at low tide, vast areas of mudflats provide a happy hunting ground for thousands of wading birds. The Severn estuary is no exception. At Severn Beach, where a railway was built in an attempt to turn this desolate resort into Bristol's Blackpool, the fine views extend across the open mud flats towards South Wales and the Forest of Dean. Closer to hand is the Second Severn Crossing, built between 1992 and 1996 to relieve the pressure on the ageing original Severn Bridge. North of Severn Beach is New Passage, where a truncated pier marks the site of the terminus of the former South Wales Union Railway. It was from here that passengers would disembark for ferries to Portskewett in Wales prior to the opening of the Severn Tunnel.

A narrow inlet amongst the dunes and mudflats

1 Walk to the end of **Station Road**, and head up onto the promenade that runs alongside the **Severn Estuary**. Turn right and follow the promenade for just under 1 mile to the remains of an old pier at **New Passage**, passing under the **Second Seven Crossing** along the way. Continue along the promenade for 100 yards to a point where the path bears right to a seat, just past a number of properties on the right. This is a convenient resting place at the halfway point on the walk, with fine views up the river towards the first **Severn Bridge**.

GRADE: 1
ESTIMATED CALORIE BURN: 125

Distance: 2 miles
Stiles: None
Terrain: A level walk along the Severn that essentially follows the riverside promenade.
Time: 1½ hours
Map: OS Explorer 154
Starting point: GR 540848
Directions to Start / Parking / Public Transport: Follow the A403 south from the M48 towards Avonmouth for 5 miles, before turning right towards Severn Beach. In ½ mile, bear left into Station Road and park on the roadside in the vicinity of the station. Severn Beach is served by a regular rail service from Bristol Temple Meads. Note, however, that the trains terminate at Avonmouth on a Sunday.
Refreshments: Shirley's Café in Station Road at Severn Beach is as old-fashioned and traditional a café as can be found anywhere.

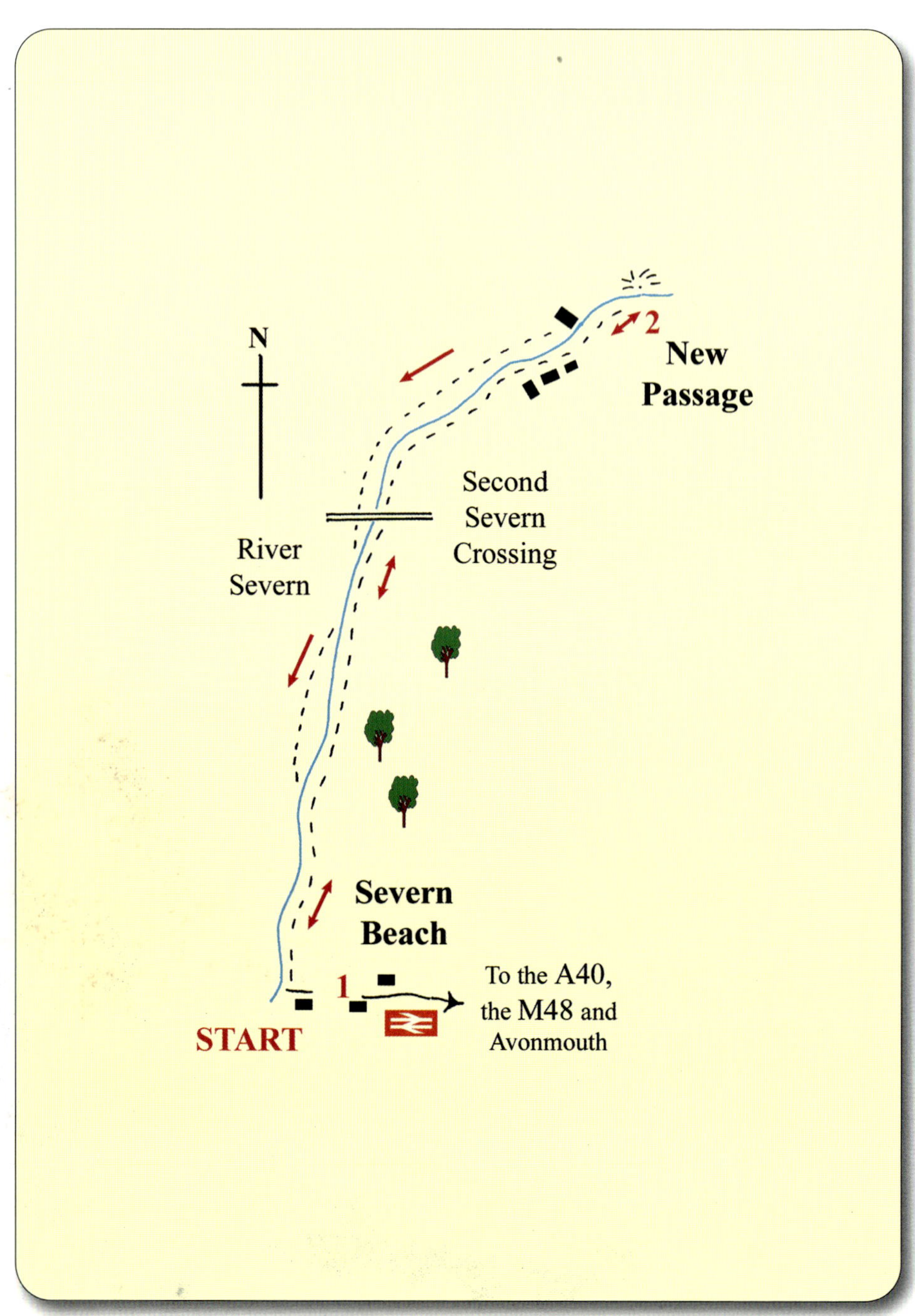

N
2
New Passage
Second Severn Crossing
River Severn
Severn Beach
1
To the A40, the M48 and Avonmouth
START

■ *Fishing on Severn Beach* ■

2 Turn around, and follow the promenade back towards **Severn Beach**. A few paces beyond the remains of the pier at **New Passage**, veer right onto a concrete path that runs alongside the foreshore. Keep on this path until it rejoins the promenade just beyond the **Second Severn Crossing**. Follow the promenade for 150 yards and, just past a radar, veer right onto another concrete path running along the foreshore. Continue on this path for 200 yards until it rejoins the main path, and continue along the promenade to a point above **Station Road**. Drop back downhill to return to your vehicle.

6 Clevedon and the Bristol Channel Coast

A Walk for Poets

■ *Clevedon's splendid pier viewed from the path* ■

There is nothing that can beat a day at the coast, with rocks and pebbles, waves and sea views. This walk is based around Clevedon, a traditional Victorian seaside resort overlooking the Bristol Channel. From the promenade, the route climbs onto Church Hill and Wain's Hill, an upland area that forms a headland to the south of the town, before following a tarmac path around the headland itself. Designated as 'The Poet's Walk' because Coleridge particularly enjoyed it when he resided in the town, the views across the Channel towards Wales and along the promenade to the local pier will inspire even the most unpoetic into verse! If there is time at journey's end, continue along the promenade to the local pier, the only fully intact Grade I listed pier in the country. Poet John Betjeman once wrote that 'Clevedon without its pier would be a diamond with a flaw'.

The view from the headland

1 Walk across to the promenade beyond the **Little Harp**, and turn left. At the far end of the promenade, climb the steps into the woodland to begin following **'The Poet's Walk'**. Ignoring any side turnings, climb to the top of **Church Hill** where the tree cover is left behind and open views begin to appear. Cross to the far side of the hilltop, and follow a path on the left down to a tarmac path. Follow this path to the right along to **St Andrew's church**, and continue down to **Old Church Road**.

GRADE: 1
ESTIMATED CALORIE BURN: 200

Distance: 2 miles
Stiles: None
Terrain: Level walking along the promenade, with gentle climbs onto Church Hill and Wain's Hill.
Time: 1½ hours
Map: OS Explorer 154
Starting point: GR 339714
Directions to Start / Parking / Public Transport: From junction 20 of the M5 motorway, follow the signs to Clevedon's sea front. Within 200 yards of a sharp right turn that sees the road heading parallel to the foreshore, separated from it by a large grassed play area, park on the roadside by the Little Harp Inn. *First* run a regular bus service from Bristol to Clevedon.
Refreshments: There are several pubs and cafés on Clevedon's seafront, including the Little Harp at journey's end.

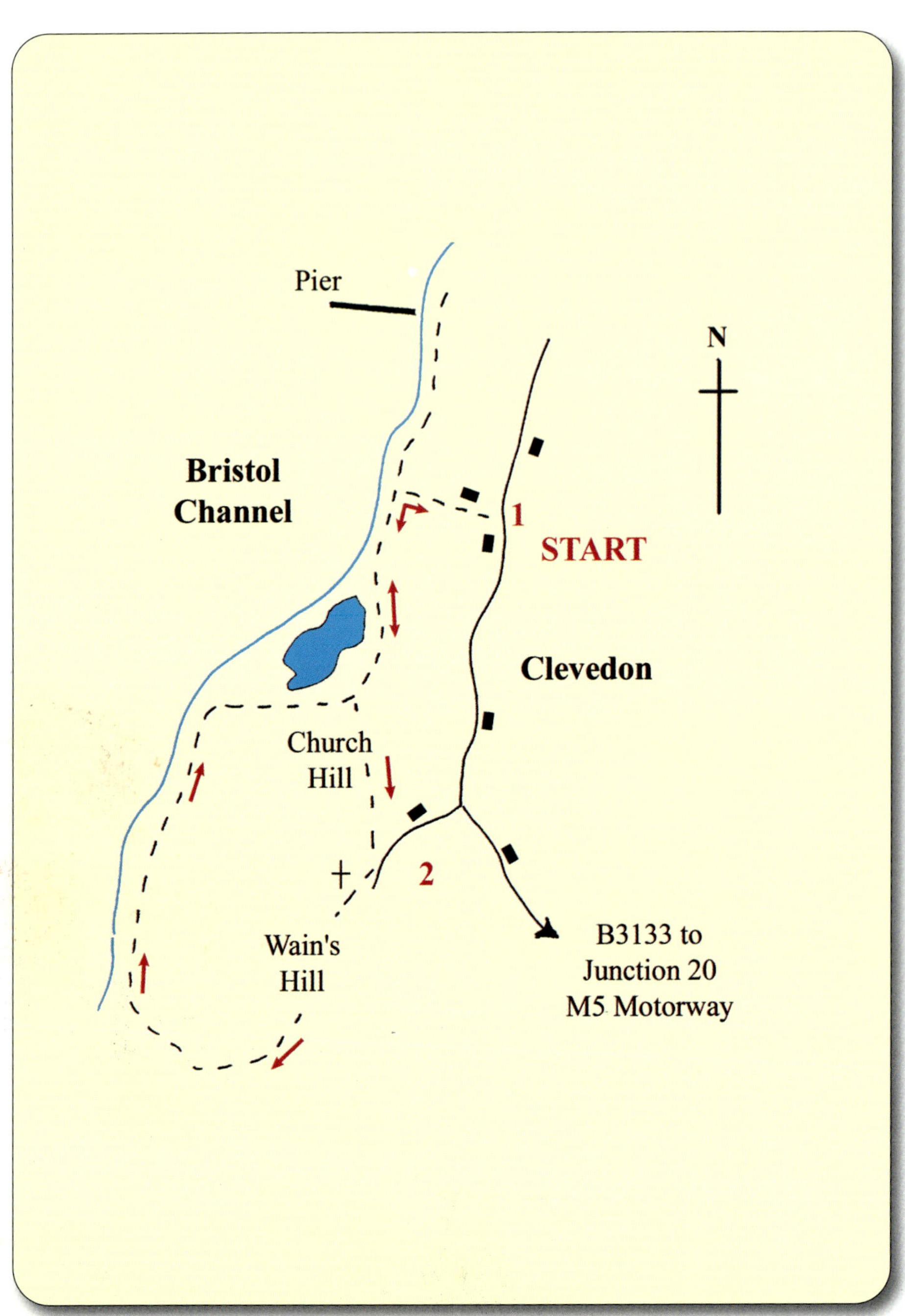
Pier
N
Bristol Channel
1
START
Clevedon
Church Hill
2
Wain's Hill
B3133 to Junction 20 M5 Motorway

■ *The entrance to the pier* ■

2 Turn right and, in 200 yards, pass through a gateway, a small boatyard ahead. Almost immediately, turn right onto the path that climbs **Wain's Hill**. Follow this path to the south-western tip of the headland, where a seat commands views across the Channel. From the tip of the headland, continue following the path around the coast and back towards **Clevedon**. Keep on this path all the way back to the old boating lake, where the path bears to the right to rejoin the promenade. It is now a simple matter of retracing your steps to the end of the walk.

Newbridge and the River Avon

A Stroll Through the Avon Valley

FOOTPATHS FOR FITNESS

■ *The river Avon* ■

In 1794 William Matthews wrote in detail about the Avon Navigation. 'Bath is a proper inland port. Barges that have one mast and sail bring heavy goods from Bristol, and generally return laden with large blocks of freestone. The river beautifully winds on towards Bristol, in a delightful and happy vale, between verdant hills and rural villages. West of Bath it runs under a noble bridge of stone, that for height and expansion seems to rival the Rialto at Venice.' This was none other than Newbridge, the starting point for this delightful stroll through the Avon valley, that also follows a short section of the Bristol and Bath Railway Path. Built on the bed of the former Midland Railway that ran between Bath and Bristol, this victim of the Beeching cuts is now one of the most popular leisure routes in the whole region.

■ *The colourful marina* ■

1 Walk along to **Newbridge** and, immediately before crossing the **river Avon**, follow a stepped path on the right downhill. At the bottom of the steps, turn left and walk underneath **Newbridge**. Follow the riverside path for 200 yards to an old bridge that carries the Railway Path. Pass underneath the bridge before turning left up to the Railway Path. Turn left, cross the **Avon** and follow the path ahead for ¾ mile to a bridge across the river.

GRADE: 1
ESTIMATED CALORIE BURN: 200

Distance: 2 miles
Stiles: None
Terrain: A flat level walk – just a few steps up onto the Railway Path and down to the river Avon – that is a perfect walk for anybody starting to walk for fitness.
Time: 1½ hours
Map: OS Explorer 155
Starting point: GR 717658
Directions to Start / Parking / Public Transport: Newbridge lies on the A4, 2 miles east of Bath city centre. Leave your car in the parking area alongside the main road on the Bath side of the river Avon. *First* run a regular bus service from Bath to Bristol that passes within a short distance of the start of the walk.
Refreshments: The Boathouse at Newbridge enjoys an enviable location overlooking the river Avon. It is also conveniently located at journey's end.

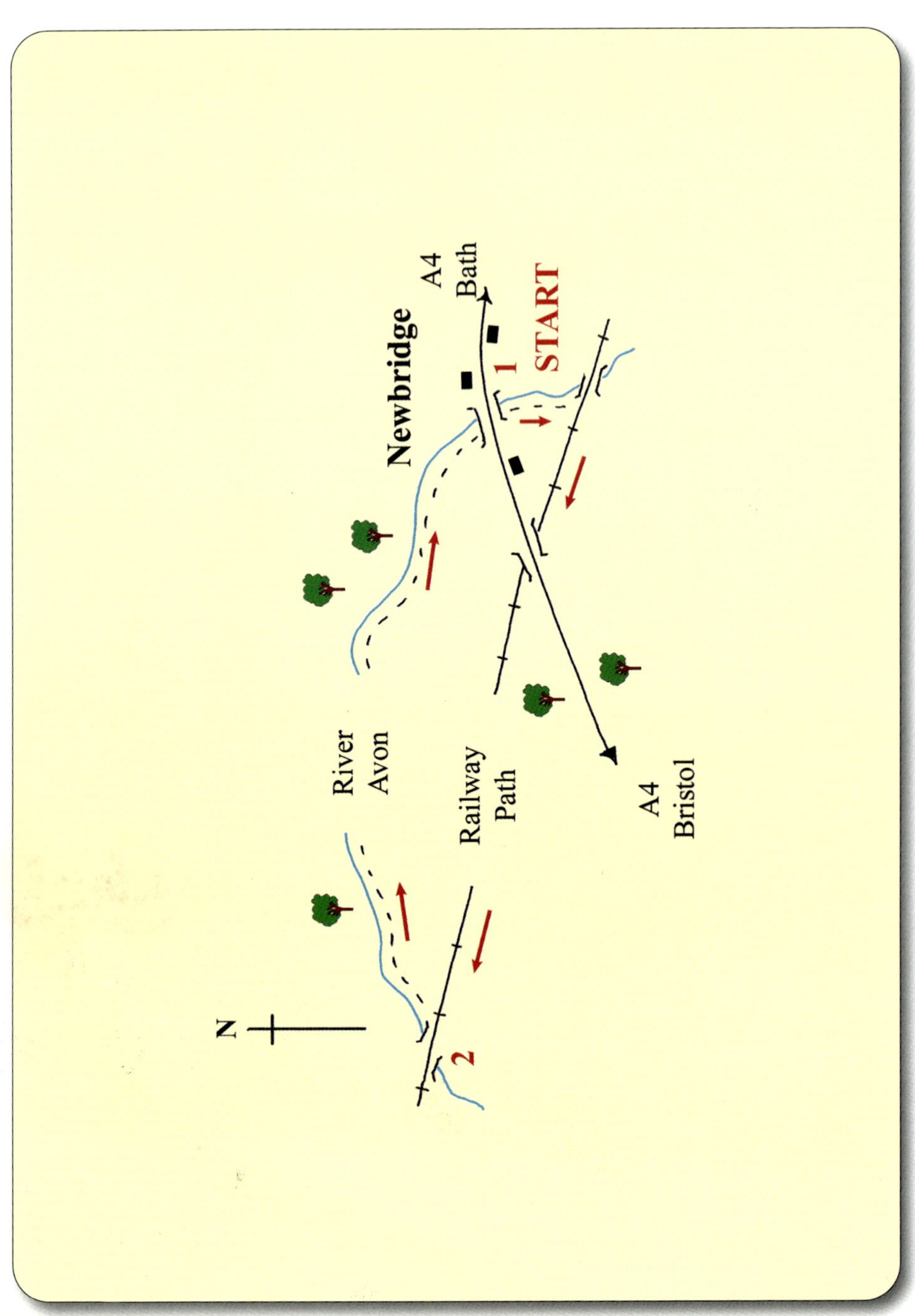
A4
Bath
Newbridge
START
1
River
Avon
Railway
Path
A4
Bristol
N
2

■ *The Bristol and Bath Railway Path built on the bed of the former Midland Railway* ■

2 Just before this bridge, follow a stepped path on the right down to the riverbank. Turn right, and follow the river upstream across two fields. At the far side of the second field, continue along the riverside path. A water board enclosure is in the trees on the right. Beyond this enclosure, follow an access road ahead along to **Newbridge**, climb some steps to reach the A4 and turn left to cross the river and return to the parking area.

8 Dyrham and Hinton Hill

An Ancient Landscape

■ *The church at Dyrham* ■

Dyrham is best known for its grand 17th-century mansion – now a National Trust property – set within a large landscaped garden and a deer park. There is also a rather pretty village, where handsome stone cottages stand against a backdrop of the Cotswold escarpment. Across the fields stands Hinton Hill, where the humps and bumps on the ground mark the site of an ancient hill fort. The Anglo-Saxon Chronicle tells us that the invading Saxons under Cuthwine and Ceawlin fought against the Britons and slew three kings, Coinmail, Condidan and Farimail on the lonely hillside. With far-ranging views across the Severn Vale towards Wales, this is a walk with interest and intrigue at every turn.

■ *The Cotswold Way* ■

1 Walk east along the main street to a junction at the bottom and turn right along the lane to **Hinton**. In 250 yards, turn right at a junction and, in 40 yards, by a chestnut tree, follow a waymarked path on the left to a stile. Cross a narrow field to a gateway opposite and, in the following field, walk ahead to another gateway. Bear half right in the next field to a stile in the top right corner and join **Cock Lane**. Turn right, and follow this lane for 300 yards to its junction with **Hinton Hill**. Turn right and, in 25 yards, cross a stile on the right.

GRADE: 1
ESTIMATED CALORIE BURN: 200

Distance: 2 miles
Stiles: 4
Terrain: This walk has one or two gentle climbs along the way, especially the section along Cock Lane that climbs towards Hinton Hill. There is nothing too demanding, however, and the compensation is a downhill section back into Dyrham.
Time: 1½ hours
Map: OS Explorer 155
Starting point: GR 739757
Directions to Start / Parking / Public Transport: Follow the A46 north from its junction with the A420 at Cold Ashton for 2 miles, before turning left to follow a lane downhill into Dyrham village. On entering the village, pass a right turn to the church and continue into the main street. Park, with consideration, on the roadside. There is no regular bus service to the village of Dyrham.
Refreshments: At journey's end, drive up to the A46 and turn left. In just 200 yards, the Tollgate Tea Rooms is located alongside the main road.

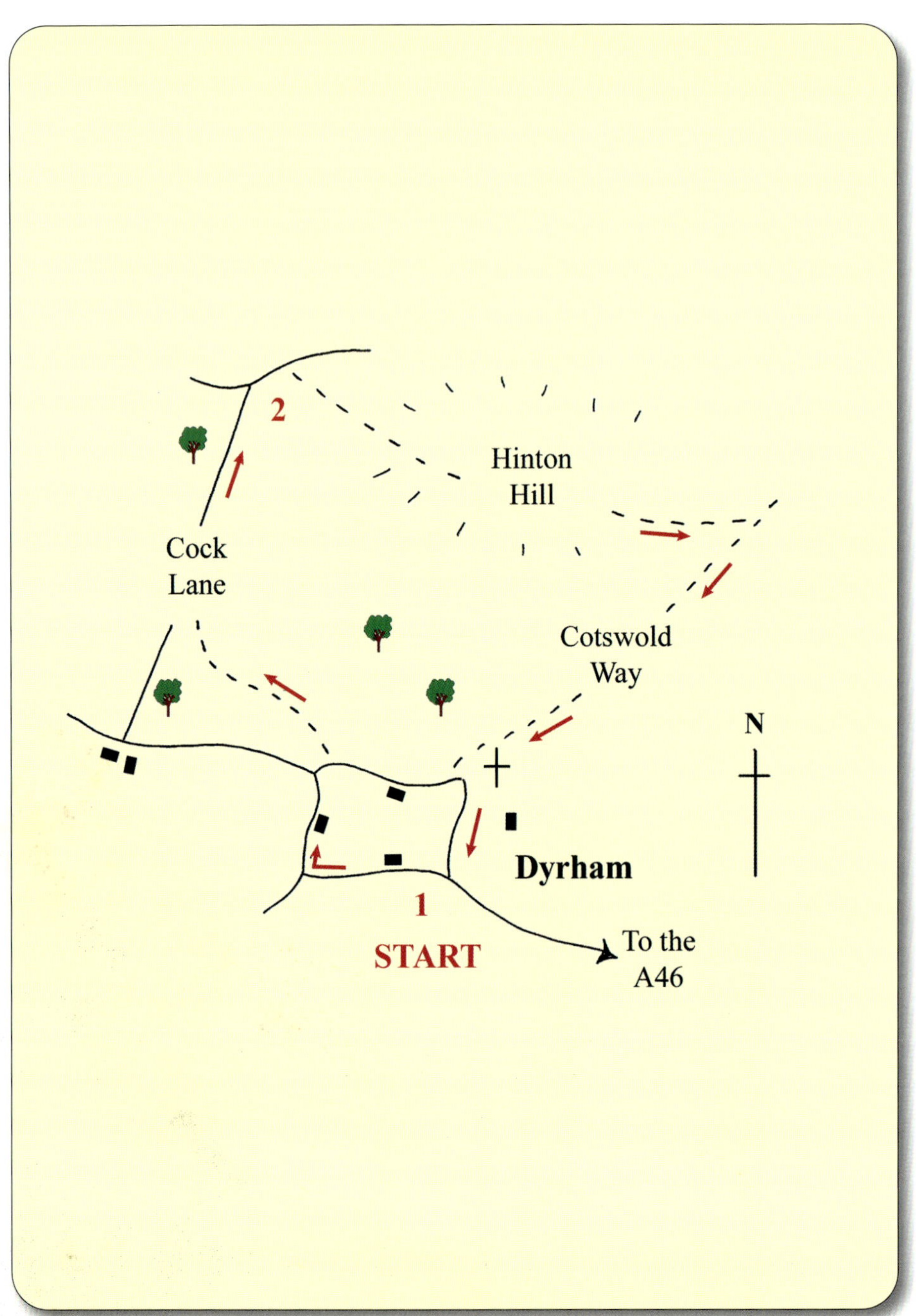
2
Hinton
Hill
Cock
Lane
Cotswold
Way
N
Dyrham
1
START
To the
A46

■ *Dyrham House, a 17th-century mansion* ■

2 Turn left and walk across the top of **Hinton Hill**. On the far side of the hilltop, pass to the right of a rampart before continuing to a gateway in the right corner of the hilltop enclosure. Follow the right edge of the following field to a stile, before heading uphill across the middle of an open field to reach the boundary wall of **Dyrham Park** on its far side. Turn right along part of the **Cotswold Way** and follow the left edges of the next four fields to a gate at the far end of the fourth field. Continue along a track down to the road in **Dyrham**. Turn left, and follow the lane along past the village church and **Dyrham House** to reach a road junction in 250 yards. Turn right back into Dyrham's main street.

9 Hambrook and the Frome Valley

FOOTPATHS FOR FITNESS

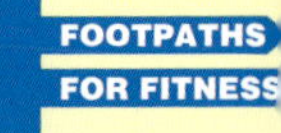

By Village and Hill Fort

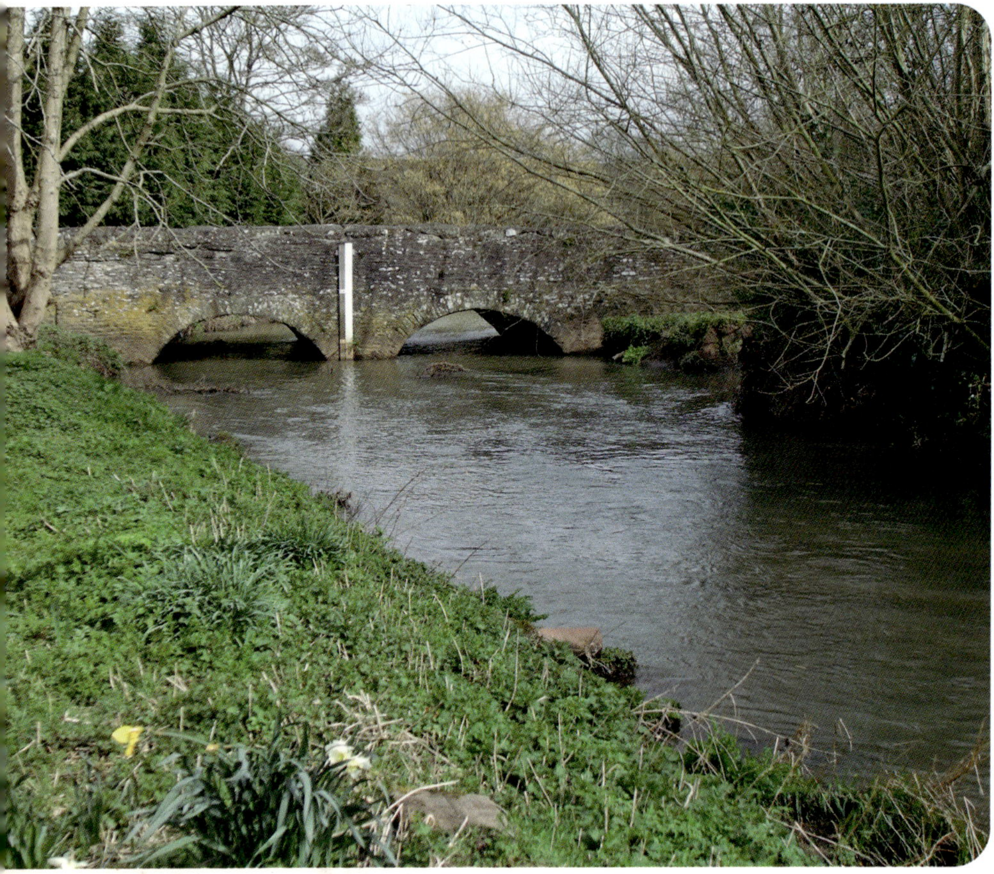

■ *Bridge over the river Frome* ■

Hambrook is quite literally the 'hamlet on the brook', and a pretty place it is too, despite the intrusion of the M4 motorway. There is a vast open common – home to the local football and cricket teams – a grand old chapel, handsome cottages, a village school and some fine walking along the river Frome. Above the village lies Bury Hill, the site of an Iron Age hill fort, which was subsequently occupied and modified by the Romans. Quarrying was historically the mainstay of the village, with the path through the Dingle passing former rock faces, now reverting to nature with an abundance of tree and shrub cover. It was rumoured that any itinerant labourer able to erect a cottage overnight – with smoke issuing forth from its chimney – was to be granted squatter's rights in this area. This is a remarkably rural excursion for an area so close to the Bristol conurbation.

1 Facing the chapel, turn left and walk downhill. At the bottom of the hill, where the main road bears right, keep ahead along the cul de sac between the **Hambrook Inn** and the **White Horse**. In 30 yards, just before the bridge over the **Bradley Brook**, turn left through a hand gate to follow the **Frome Valley Walkway**. In 200 yards, where this track joins a lane, turn right, cross the **Frome** and walk around a left-hand bend to a junction. Follow the lane ahead, with the **Frome** on the left, for 150 yards to the next junction. Keep ahead, ignoring a left turn to Winterbourne, and walk up past **Moorend Farm** to a crossroads. Turn left towards **Winterbourne** and drop downhill to a junction. Turn right and, in 50 yards, turn right to follow a waymarked footpath uphill through woodland to some steps and the entrance to **Camp Cottage**.

GRADE: 2
ESTIMATED CALORIE BURN: 300

Distance: 3 miles
Stiles: 4
Terrain: A generally level walk, with just one or two climbs along the way. There is a short but sharp ascent through woodland to reach Bury Hill Camp, and another climb up Mill Steps to reach Winterbourne Down church. The paths alongside the river Frome could prove muddy following heavy rainfall.
Time: 2 hours
Map: OS Explorer 155
Starting point: GR 645793
Directions to Start / Parking / Public Transport: Follow the B4058 towards Hambrook from the Bristol Ring Road just east of the M32. Follow this road for ¾ mile, passing under the M4 motorway, before bearing left up Whiteshill. At the top of the hill, park in the lay-by on the right opposite the chapel. *First* run regular buses from Bristol to Hambrook.
Refreshments: At the end of the walk, the White Horse Inn lies at the bottom of Whiteshill in Hambrook.

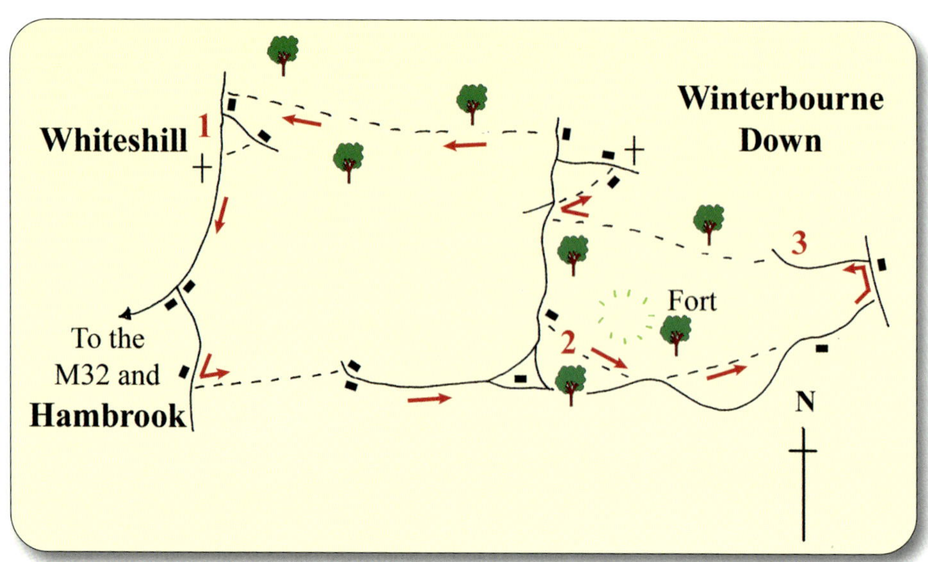

■ *The village of Hambrook seen from the route* ■

■ *The chapel at Hambrook* ■

2 Pass in front of this property to a stile, pass through an area of scrubland and enter the enclosure of **Bury hill fort**. Cross the enclosure, pass through the rampart opposite, cross a stile and join a lane. Turn right down to a road junction and turn left. In 70 yards, on a right-hand bend, cross the stile ahead and follow the left edge of the field ahead to a stile in the far corner. Join a lane and follow this lane to the left downhill to a junction by a green. Turn left and continue down to a junction with an unclassified road. Turn left and follow this busy road over **Damson's Bridge** before turning immediately left into the Dingle. Follow this lane for 200 yards before veering left by a whitewashed cottage onto a footpath – the **Frome Valley Walkway**.

3 Follow this path for 200 yards to a footbridge on the left. Cross the **Frome**, turn right and, with the river on the right, continue to a lane. Turn right, cross the **Frome** and immediately keep right to **Mill House** and climb **Mill Steps** to a lane. Opposite – slightly to the right – is the entrance to

The church at Winterbourne Down

Winterbourne Down church. Turn left and walk downhill to a junction with **Mill Road**. Turn right and, in a few yards, opposite the **Old School House**, pass through a hand gate on the left. Cross the field ahead to a gate in the middle of the opposite field boundary and, in the next field, cross to a hand gate opposite at the right-hand end of a number of properties. Join a road, turn left and, in 50 yards, turn left into **Pye Corner**. Follow this lane uphill to **Whiteshill Common**, before crossing the common to the parking area by the chapel.

10 Old Sodbury and the Cotswold Edge

A Walk along the Edge

■ *The view from the Cotswold Edge* ■

GRADE: 2
ESTIMATED CALORIE BURN: 250

Distance: 2½ miles
Stiles: 8
Terrain: Level fieldpaths, with one stiff climb onto the Cotswold hilltops. Having explored Sodbury Fort, there is a parallel descent down the Cotswold edge. The walk presents a greater number of stiles compared to earlier walks, adding to its challenge!
Time: 2 hours
Map: OS Explorer 167
Starting point: GR 757818
Directions to Start / Parking / Public Transport: Old Sodbury lies on the A432 just east of Chipping Sodbury. In the centre of the village, opposite the Dog Inn, turn into Cotswold Lane. Drive up to its junction with Church Lane and turn left to park by the church. Old Sodbury is not served by a regular bus service.
Refreshments: The Dog Inn at Old Sodbury is on the A342 at the junction with Cotswold Lane.

Running the length of its hill range is the Cotswold Escarpment, known colloquially as the Cotswold Edge. This is the divide between the hilltops and the Severn Vale, a slope with a view! Old Sodbury lies in the lee of the Cotswold Edge, and there can be few better churchyard seats than the one found at St John's in the village. The church enjoys a slight elevation with a grand outlook across the Severn towards the distant Welsh hills. North of Old Sodbury lies Little Sodbury, with another fine church that has connections with William Tyndale. Whilst employed as a tutor in the village, Tyndale started work on his translation of the Bible into English. On the hilltop above these neighbouring villages we find Sodbury Fort, a site of multi-occupancy and one of the finest hill forts in the Cotswold region. Cotswold stone villages, fine views, ancient churches and a hilltop antiquity all combine to form a perfect short stroll in the Southwolds.

1 Follow the path through the churchyard to a gate in the boundary wall, passing the church on the right. Beyond this gate, drop downhill to the bottom left corner of a hillside field, before turning right to walk alongside the bottom field boundary. Towards the far side of the field, pass to the right of a pond and continue to a stile in the end field boundary. Follow the right edges of the next four fields to reach a stile in the far right corner of

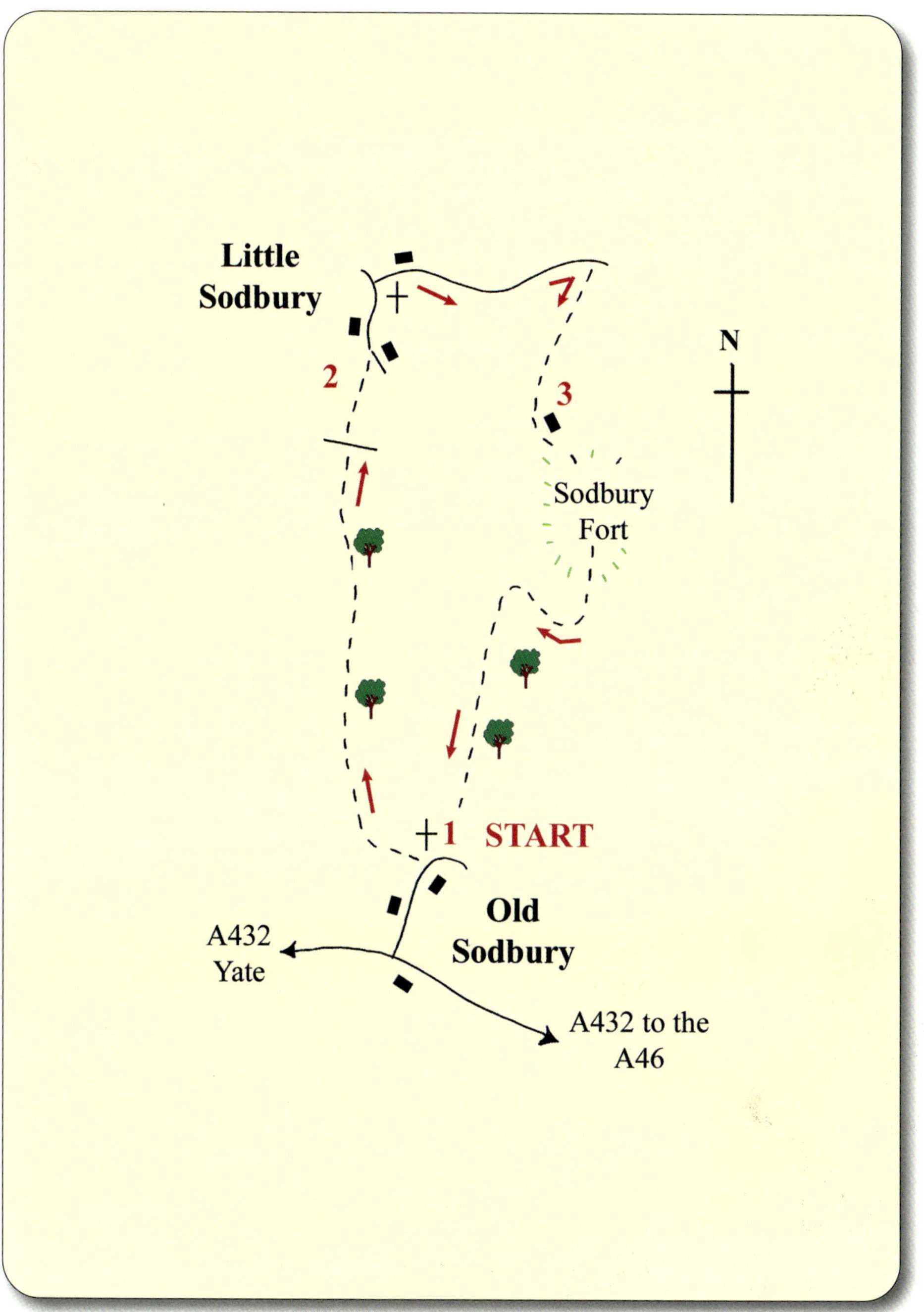
Little
Sodbury
2
3
N
Sodbury
Fort
1
START
Old
Sodbury
A432
Yate
A432 to the
A46

the fourth field, and a lane. Cross the lane to climb a stile opposite, before crossing to a stile in the far right corner of the field ahead.

2 On the lane in **Little Sodbury**, turn left and walk past the village church to a junction by a small green. Turn right, and follow a lane uphill – signposted to Horton – for ¼ mile to a road junction on the hilltop. Cross a stile on the right and head diagonally across the field to its far right corner. Pass through a hand gate and walk down the right edge of the lawn alongside a barn conversion to a gravelled parking area. Pass through a gate on the right at this point, and follow a grassy path along the right edge of the converted farm buildings.

3 Some 40 yards beyond the barn conversion, pass through a hand gate on the left, walk ahead for 25 yards and turn right to pass through the ramparts of **Sodbury Fort**. Cross the enclosure ahead, pass through a gap in the ramparts opposite and continue across the hilltop field to a hand gate.

■ *Just the spot for a welcome rest!* ■

■ *Sodbury hillfort* ■

Beyond this gate, follow the path ahead that soon bears right and drops downhill through woodland. At the bottom of the hill, turn left to a hand gate before following the top left edge of an open field across to a hand gate in its far left corner. Walk ahead across the next field to another hand gate and continue down an enclosed path to the junction of **Cotswold Lane** and **Church Lane** in **Old Sodbury**. Turn right back to the church.

Bradford-on-Avon and Avoncliff

By River and Canal

■ *Bradford-on-Avon is a town full of interest* ■

Bradford-on-Avon is a delightful place, that regularly features in those lists of Britain's best small towns. Stone cottages that date back to the heyday of the West of England's woollen trade line the hillside above the river Avon, presenting a picture that has been described as 'Bath in miniature'. The river is followed across a series of meadows to Avoncliff, a remote hamlet where a handsome aqueduct carries the Kennet and Avon Canal across the Avon itself. Steep hillsides come tumbling down to the riverbank, presenting a perfect picture of the English landscape. The return to Bradford-on-Avon is quite simply a gentle stroll along the canal towpath, where barges and pleasure craft gently make their way up and down what is southern Britain's finest waterway.

■ *The Lock Inn Cottage beside the Kennet and Avon* ■

1 Walk along to the far end of the station car park and follow a path that drops downhill to the **river Avon**. Keep on this path as it bears left to pass under a railway bridge, before continuing across a grassy recreation area to join a path by an ancient packhorse bridge. Do not cross the river – instead, follow the tarmac path ahead, the **Avon** on the right-hand side.

GRADE: 2
ESTIMATED CALORIE BURN: 350

Distance: 3½ miles
Stiles: None
Terrain: Level field paths and canal towpath, with just one short climb – a flight of steps up to the Kennet and Avon Canal from the riverbank.
Time: 2 hours
Map: OS Explorer 156
Starting point: GR 824607
Directions to Start / Parking / Public Transport: Bradford-on-Avon lies on the A363 road running from Bath to Trowbridge, just 2 miles from Trowbridge itself. Follow the signs to the railway station, and park in the station car park. Bradford-on-Avon and Avoncliff are both served by a regular rail service from both Bath and Bristol.
Refreshments: Refreshments can be enjoyed in the gardens of the Madhatter Tea Room in Avoncliff, or sitting alongside the Kennet and Avon Canal in Bradford at the Lock Inn Cottage, where the walk joins the B3109.

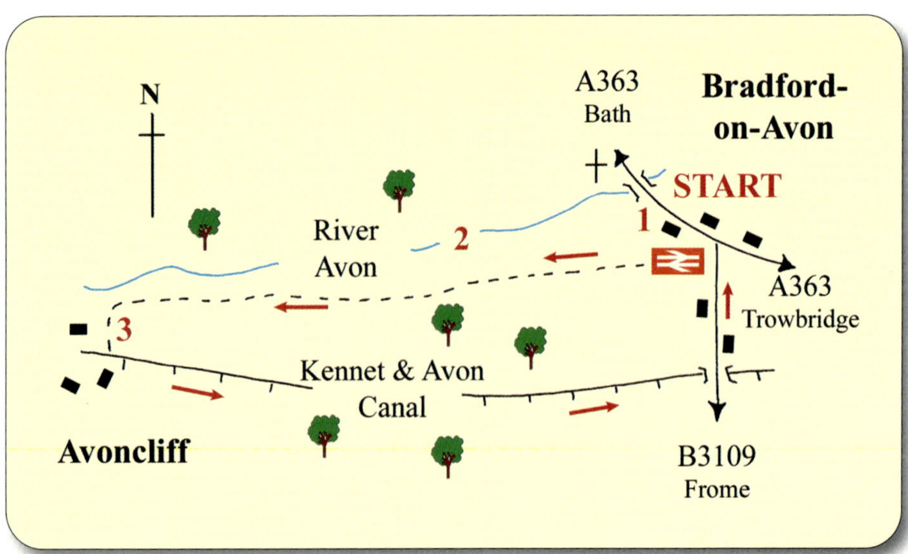

■ *Bridge Street, Bradford-on-Avon* ■

■ *The path leading under the viaduct at Avoncliff* ■

2 In 600 yards, leave the tarmac path where it bears left up to the canal and keep following a path that runs alongside the river, a water board installation on the left. Continue along a track to a gate, before following a riverside path for just over ½ mile to a weir in **Avoncliff**. Bear left at this point, and climb some steps up to the **Kennet and Avon Canal**.

3 Follow the towpath to the right to explore Avoncliff – *for the main walk*, turn left and follow the towpath for 1½ miles to join the B3109 in **Bradford-on-Avon**. Turn left back towards the town centre and, in 250 yards, turn left back into the station car park.

Keynsham and the Avon Valley Railway

Stepping Back In Time

■ *View from the path alongside the Avon Valley Railway* ■

Riverside walking always holds a particular appeal, especially a navigable waterway with pleasure craft making their lazy way up and down the river. The Avon at Keynsham has long been navigable and is a popular destination for local boating enthusiasts. This walk will also allow you to engage in a little nostalgia, with part of the route following the Avon Valley Railway running between Bitton and a recently-opened station named Avon Riverside. Plan your walk at the right time and you will see a steam train arrive at the station with passengers disembarking for a cruise on the river. The whole is set against a backdrop of some rather fine hills – it is actually the point where the southern edge of the Cotswolds comes tumbling down to the Avon Valley – adding an element of natural interest to the human interest along the way.

■ *Boat moored on the bank of the Avon* ■

1 Facing the **Lock Keeper Inn**, cross a stile on the left-hand side of the road and follow a path signposted to **Swineford**. Follow this path as it runs between the marina on the left and the **river Avon** on the right, through to an access lane. Follow this lane to the right, cross a cattle grid and continue across a field to a

GRADE: 2
ESTIMATED CALORIE BURN: 350

Distance: 3½ miles
Stiles: 5
Terrain: Level field paths, as well as a level tarmac path along the Avon Valley Railway. There is one short flight of steps up the railway embankment to join the railway path.
Time: 2 hours
Map: OS Explorer 155
Starting point: GR 660690
Directions to Start / Parking / Public Transport: Follow the signposted road from the A4 Keynsham bypass into the town centre, before taking the A4175 towards Willsbridge. In 600 yards, having crossed the river Avon, turn right along a side turning leading to Port Avon Marina. Turn right in front of the marina building and park on the roadside leading up to the Lock Keeper Inn. Keynsham has a railway station, close to the start of the walk, that is served by a regular service running from Bristol to Bath. Leave the station, turn right along the A4175 and it is just a few minutes' walk to the Lock Keeper Inn.
Refreshments: The Lock Keeper Inn, with lovely riverside gardens, lies at the end of the walk.

junction, where a pipe crosses the river. Continue ahead along the lane towards a whitewashed property called **Avondale House**. On reaching the house, continue ahead across the field to a gate in the end field boundary to the right of a telegraph pole.

2 Follow the left edges of two fields, before passing through a gate on the left in the corner of the second field. Continue along an enclosed section of path to a footbridge and hand gate, ignoring one slightly earlier hand gate on the left. Cross the next field to a stone outbuilding opposite and follow the hedgerow beyond this building for 40 yards to a pair of gates in the hedgerow on the right. Follow the left edge of the next field to a gate in the corner of the field, before climbing the steps opposite to reach the **Railway Path**. Turn right, and follow the path for ½ mile to a path on the right, waymarked as the **River Avon Trail**, just before **Avon Riverside Station** and a bridge over the river. (It is worth going a little further ahead to see the view of the Avon.)

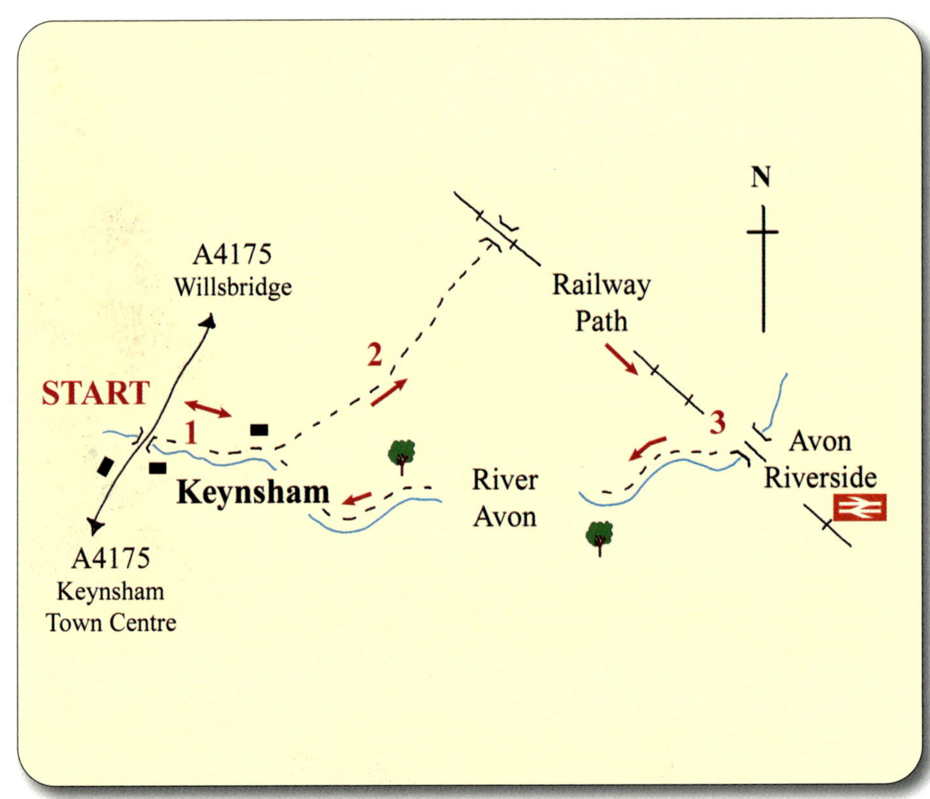

■ *A steam train on the Avon Valley Railway* ■

3 Follow a tarmac path downhill to a picnic area by the river, turn right to a footbridge over the **river Boyd** and pass through a hand gate into a riverside field. With the river on the left, follow the river downstream for 1 mile across six fields to reach the pipe across the river passed at the outset. Retrace your steps along the lane ahead back to the cattle grid and in 150 yards veer left off the lane onto a riverside path. Follow this path back to the road by the **Lock Keeper Inn**.

Stanton Prior and Newton Park

A Little Bit of a Challenge

A view of Stanton Prior

To the south-west of Bath the outlying hills of the Cotswolds and Mendips come together to form a most charming pastoral landscape. The hills are gently undulating, and are crossed by narrow winding lanes bordered by traditional hedgerows that seldom carry much traffic. Stanton Prior sits in the midst of this landscape, the tower of St Lawrence church being a prominent landmark from all around. A climb out of the village onto the nearby hilltop brings expansive views, not only of the village itself but also more distant points such as Kelston Round Hill and Lansdown. Below lies Newton Park, where the 18th-century mansion was built by the second Joseph Langton. The grounds and associated buildings now form Bath Spa University, surely one of the most attractive locations for a seat of learning in the country. This is a delightful rural excursion which is surprisingly remote given the proximity of both Bath and Bristol.

■ *St Lawrence church, Stanton Prior* ■

1 Enter the churchyard and walk around the back of the church to reach a stile in the boundary wall. Continue on an enclosed path to a hand gate and a small paddock. Cross to a hand gate in the far left-hand corner of this field. Beyond the gate, turn left and follow the line of a hedgerow on the left. In 40 yards, where this hedgerow bears left, keep walking in the same direction uphill across the open field to a hand gate in the top field boundary. Beyond the gate, follow a short section of enclosed path into a small area of woodland. Keep walking

GRADE: 2
ESTIMATED CALORIE BURN: 350

Distance: 3 miles
Stiles: 7
Terrain: A walk that presents a bit of a challenge, with a climb out of Stanton Prior, and a parallel descent to Newton Park. There are also a number of stiles to negotiate.
Time: 2 hours
Map: OS Explorer 155
Starting point: GR 678628
Directions to Start / Parking / Public Transport: Follow the A4 west from Bath for 2 miles, before turning onto the A39. In 2 miles, by the Wheatsheaf Inn, turn left and follow a narrow lane into Stanton Prior. Park on the roadside by the church. Stanton Prior has no public transport.
Refreshment stop: The lane from Stanton Prior joins the A39 by the Wheatsheaf Inn.

ahead through this woodland to a hand gate and a track. Turn right, and follow the track uphill to reach a lane on the hilltop in 250 yards.

2 Follow the lane to the left for ½ mile to a crossroads, before continuing ahead along the lane waymarked to **Newton St Loe**. In another ½ mile, cross a stile on the left and follow a footpath along to an open hilltop field. Follow the right edge of this field downhill until you reach an old concrete farm road by a small copse. Follow this old road ahead down to a stile and the playing fields of **Bath Spa University**. Beyond this stile, follow the right edge of the playing field for 50 yards to a marker post. Turn left, and walk the length of the playing field to a stile in the end field boundary.

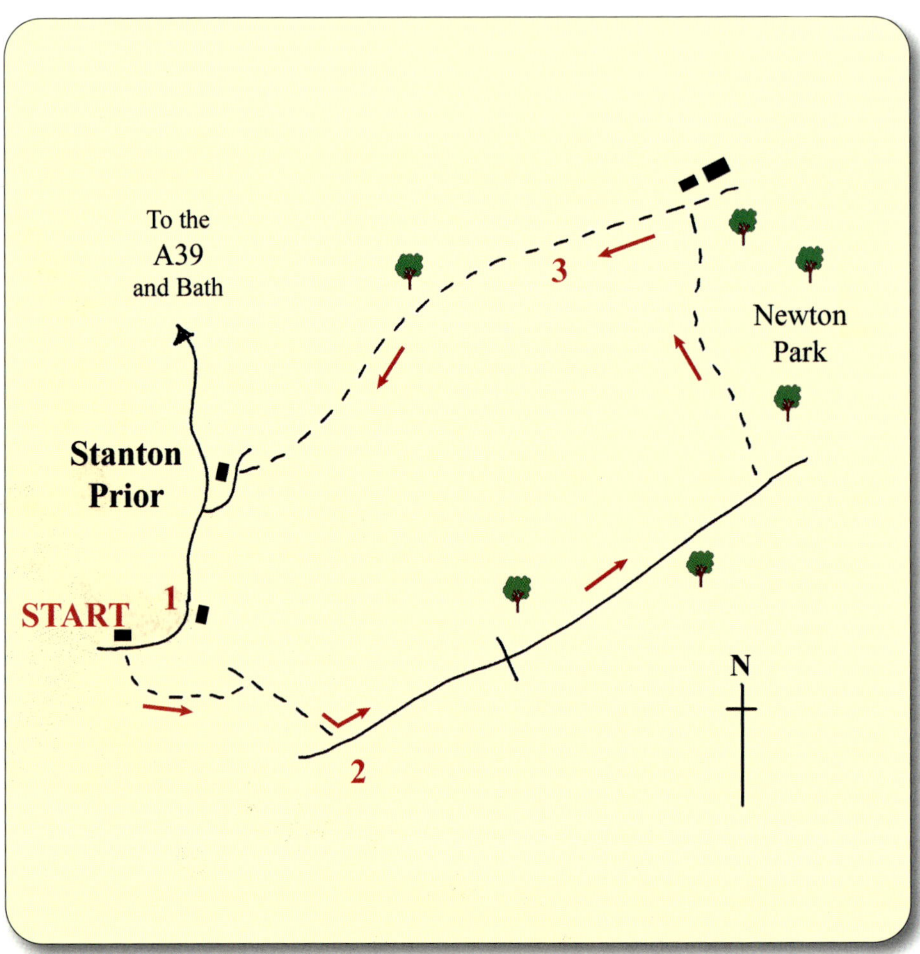

■ *The 18th-century mansion at Newton Park* ■

3 Beyond this stile, cross an open field to another stile and then cross the next field to a dip at the far end. Cross a stile in the bottom of this dip, and follow an enclosed path to a hand gate and open field. Follow the right edge of this field to a gate, a stile and a lane. Follow the lane ahead for 200 yards to a road junction, turn left and keep on the road to a junction in 200 yards. Keep on the main lane that bears right back along to **Stanton Prior church**.

14 Lansdown Hill and Langridge

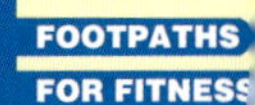

Steep Hillsides and Deep Valleys

FOOTPATHS FOR FITNESS

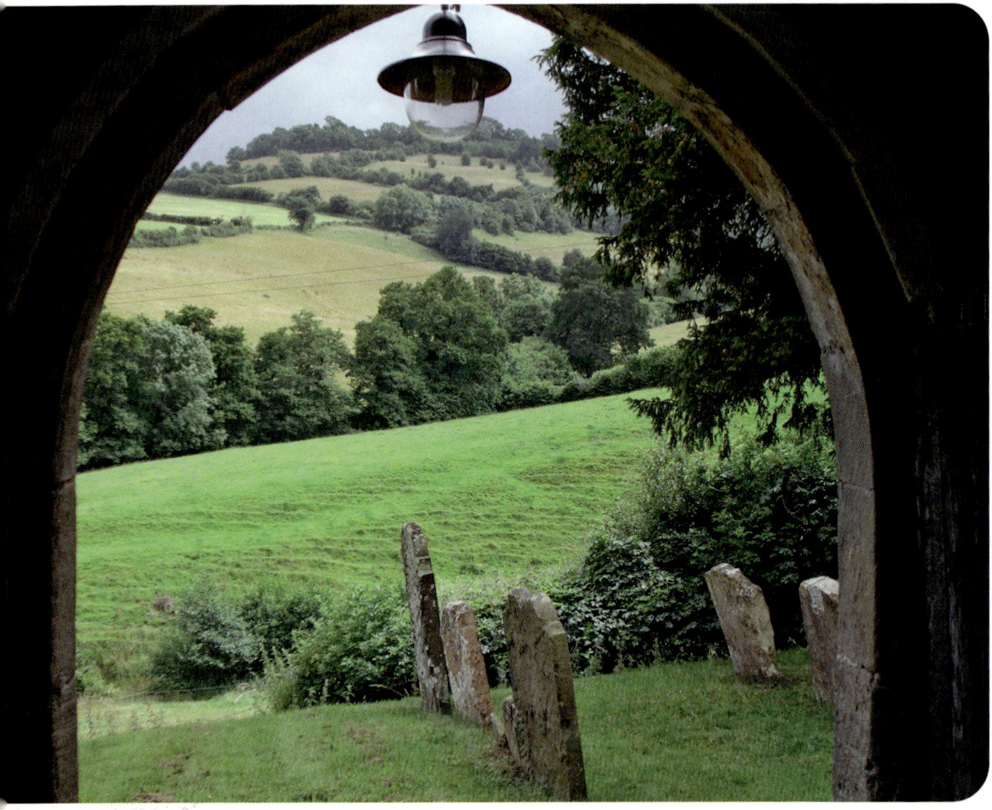

■ *View from the Langridge church porch* ■

Lansdown Hill enjoys a commanding position, high above Bath, with magnificent views across the southern Cotswold landscape. All around are steep hillsides and deep valleys, with old-fashioned farms and handsome properties, each enjoying an enviable location and outlook. It was not always this way, however, for in 1643 this was the site of a savage battle during the English Civil War. This particular skirmish has been described as a 'Pyrrhic Royalist victory', with Lord Hopton's forces suffering between 200 and 300 casualties in securing this hilltop site. Altogether more peaceful is the hamlet of Langridge, whose charming little church sits alongside the narrow and winding lane that drops into the valley bottom. With its squat Norman tower and saddleback roof – as well as its delightful setting overlooking a nearby hillside – the churchyard seat is quite the place to rest and linger awhile on this relatively challenging walk.

■ *Stained glass in Langridge church* ■

1 Walk back to the **Langridge road** and the local village hall. Cross a stone slab stile to the left of the village hall before crossing to a barn in the far right corner of the field. Pass through a gate by the tin barn, before following the right edge of the field ahead for 250 yards to a gate. Pass through this gate and, in the next field walk across to a stile in its far right corner. Beyond the stile, walk ahead across the right edge of the

GRADE: 2
ESTIMATED CALORIE BURN: 350

Distance: 3¼ miles
Stiles: 2
Terrain: Probably the most demanding walk so far, with a height difference of well over 400 ft between the top of Lansdown Hill and the valley bottom. The uphill section of the walk follows a very quiet lane, meaning that the going underfoot is never muddy or rutted.
Time: 2 hours
Map: OS Explorer 155
Starting point: GR 725690
Directions to Start / Parking / Public Transport: An unclassified road runs uphill out of Bath to the local racecourse, before dropping downhill to the A420 at Wick on the fringes of Bristol. Just north of the racecourse entrance, turn right along the lane to Langridge. Almost immediately, turn right along a slip road and park on the roadside by the village hall. There is no regular bus service.
Refreshments: Turn left – towards Bath – and it is less than a minute's drive to the Blathwayt Arms on Lansdown Hill.

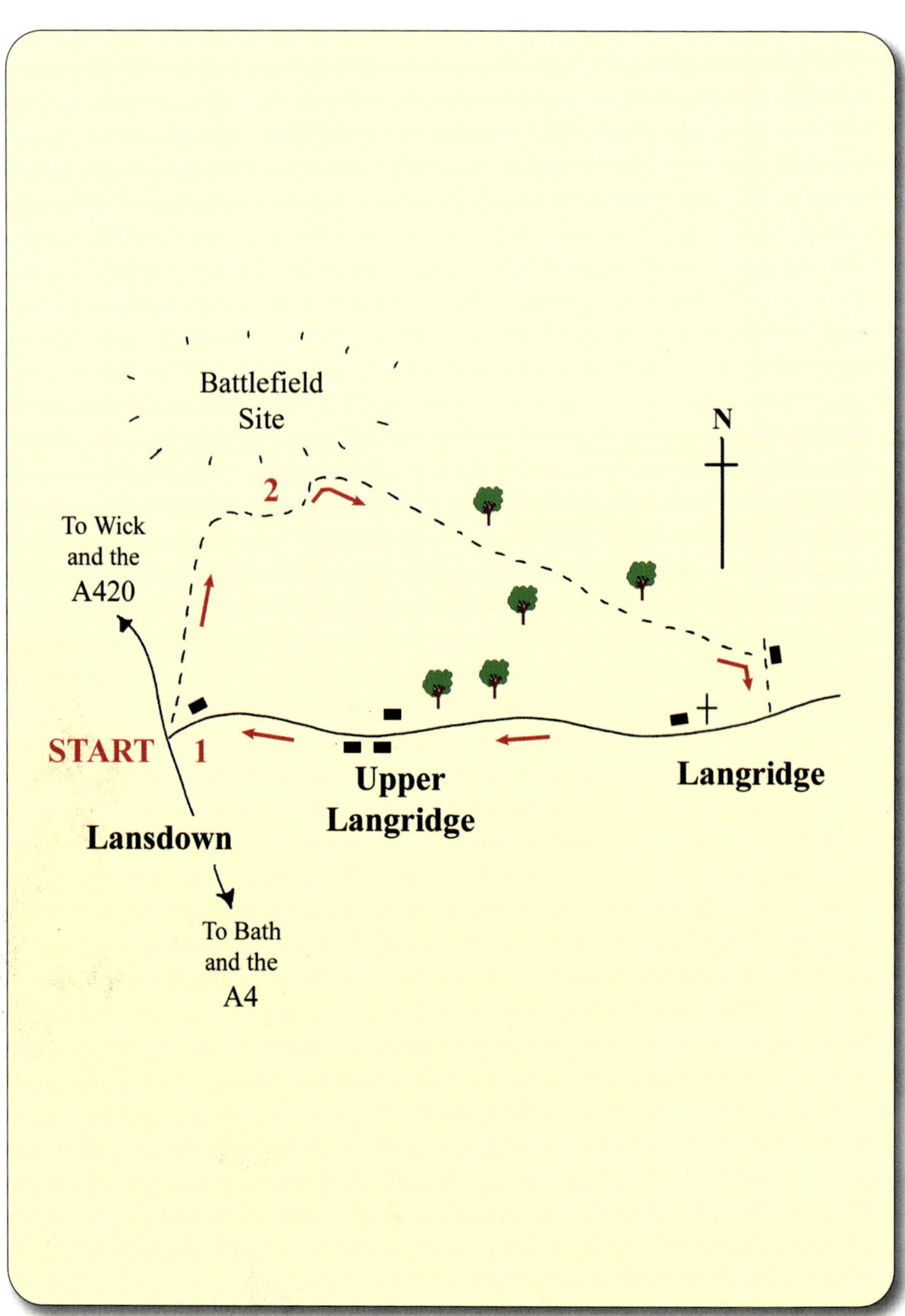
Battlefield
Site
N
2
To Wick
and the
A420
START
1
Upper
Langridge
Langridge
Lansdown
To Bath
and the
A4

■ *The wonderful Cotswold countryside* ■

field ahead – keeping to the level – to reach a gate in the right corner of the field. Follow the path ahead, keeping a wall on the left, along to a Civil War information board, a view into the local valley on the right.

2 Beyond the information board, keep on the path as it drops downhill – soon bordering a fence on the left – and continue to a gate and track. Follow this track ahead and downhill for 1 mile into the valley bottom. At a junction by a barn, turn right and continue for 350 yards to a lane. Turn right and follow this lane uphill for 150 yards to **Langridge church**. Continue along the lane for just under 1 mile back to the village hall, passing through **Upper Langridge** along the way.

15 Sea Mills and the Blaise Castle Estate

FOOTPATHS FOR FITNES

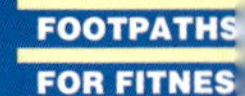

An Unexpected Landscape

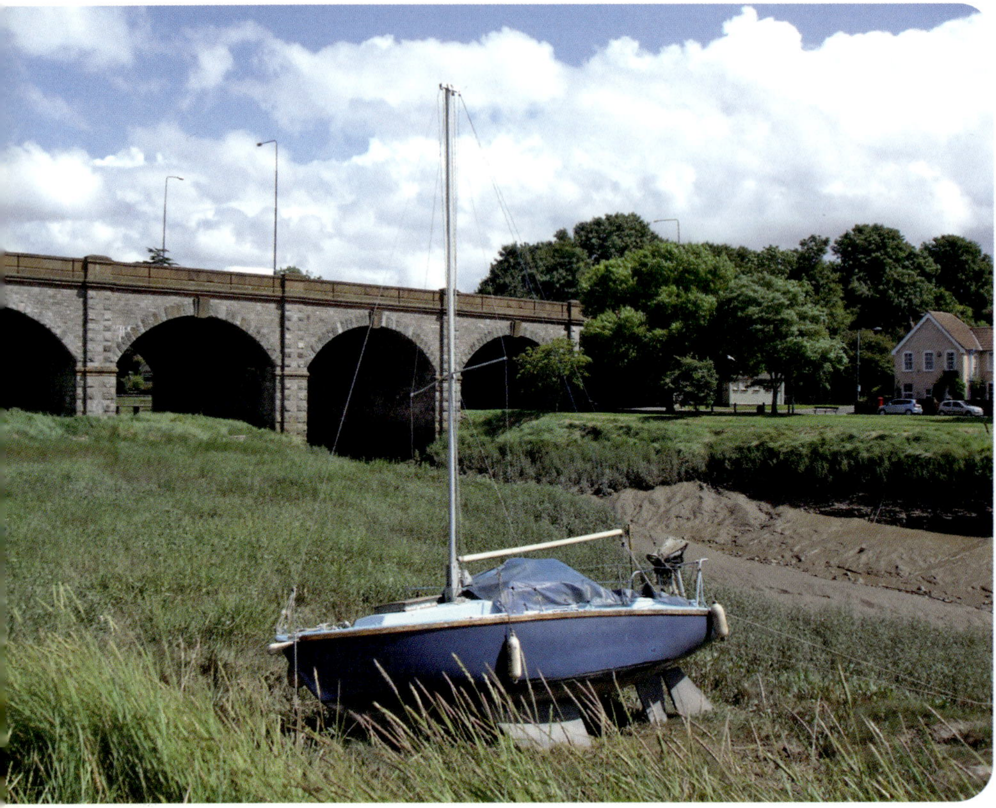

■ *Boat moored on the mudflats at Sea Mills* ■

Sea Mills may not immediately spring to mind as a walking destination. Located on the busy A4 Portway between Bristol and Avonmouth – and surrounded by sprawling housing estates – it is very much an urban landscape. Follow the river Trym, however, and a secretive wooded landscape opens up right in the heart of the city. The riverside path leads through to Combe Dingle and – the jewel in the crown – the Blaise Castle Estate. This gem of a location can boast wooded limestone cliffs, a folly castle, a grand mansion that houses a collection of artefacts depicting social history and an ancient hill fort high on Kings Weston Hill. The whole is set in grounds originally designed by Humphrey Repton. Beyond Kings Weston Hill – where the open views can only be enjoyed when there is an absence of tree cover – the route drops down through the National Trust's Shirehampton Park before reaching the tidal stretch of the river Avon. At low tide, hundreds of waders feast on the mud flats, whilst at high tide you may be lucky enough to catch a glimpse of a vessel heading to or from the City Docks in Bristol.

1 Walk along the road away from the station, passing under the bridge carrying the **A4 Portway**. Immediately after this bridge, cross a footbridge over the **river Trym** on the left. Turn right, and follow the river upstream for 300 yards to a road. Turn right, cross the river and then left up some steps to continue following the river upstream for 350 yards to reach **Shirehampton Road** – initially following a grassy meadow and latterly passing through scrubland. Turn right and, immediately past the **Mill House**, turn left into **Bell Barn Road**. Almost immediately, turn left along a footpath waymarked to the **Blaise Estate**. Shortly, at the foot of a slope, keep left at a fork and follow a path that crosses the **Trym**. Continue

GRADE: 2
ESTIMATED CALORIE BURN: 450

Distance: 4½ miles
Stiles: None
Terrain: A generally easy walk, with just one or two challenges along the way. There is a climb up to the Folly Castle – as well as onto Kings Weston Hill – but nothing too demanding. The riverbank walk alongside the tidal Avon passes through an area of long grass with no obvious path, which can be damp following heavy rain.
Time: 2½ hours
Map: OS Explorer 155
Starting point: GR 550759
Directions to Start / Parking / Public Transport: Follow the A4 Portway from Bristol towards Avonmouth for 4 miles, before taking a side turn signposted to Sea Mills station. Park on the cul de sac road leading up to the station. There is a regular railway service from Bristol to Avonmouth and Severn Beach that passes through Sea Mills.
Refreshments: If you follow the detour in point 2 of the directions, there is a café on the far side of the open parkland surrounding Blaise Castle House. It is located alongside a children's play area.

following the river upstream – the river on the right – to a bridge carrying **Dingle Road**. Pass under the bridge and continue following the woodland path ahead for 200 yards to a lane. Turn right and, in 20 yards, left into a car park.

2 Pass through the car park and follow a metalled path ahead through **Coombe Dingle** for ½ mile to a point where the path bears left over a bridge, a mill ahead. Cross the bridge, and continue on the metalled path

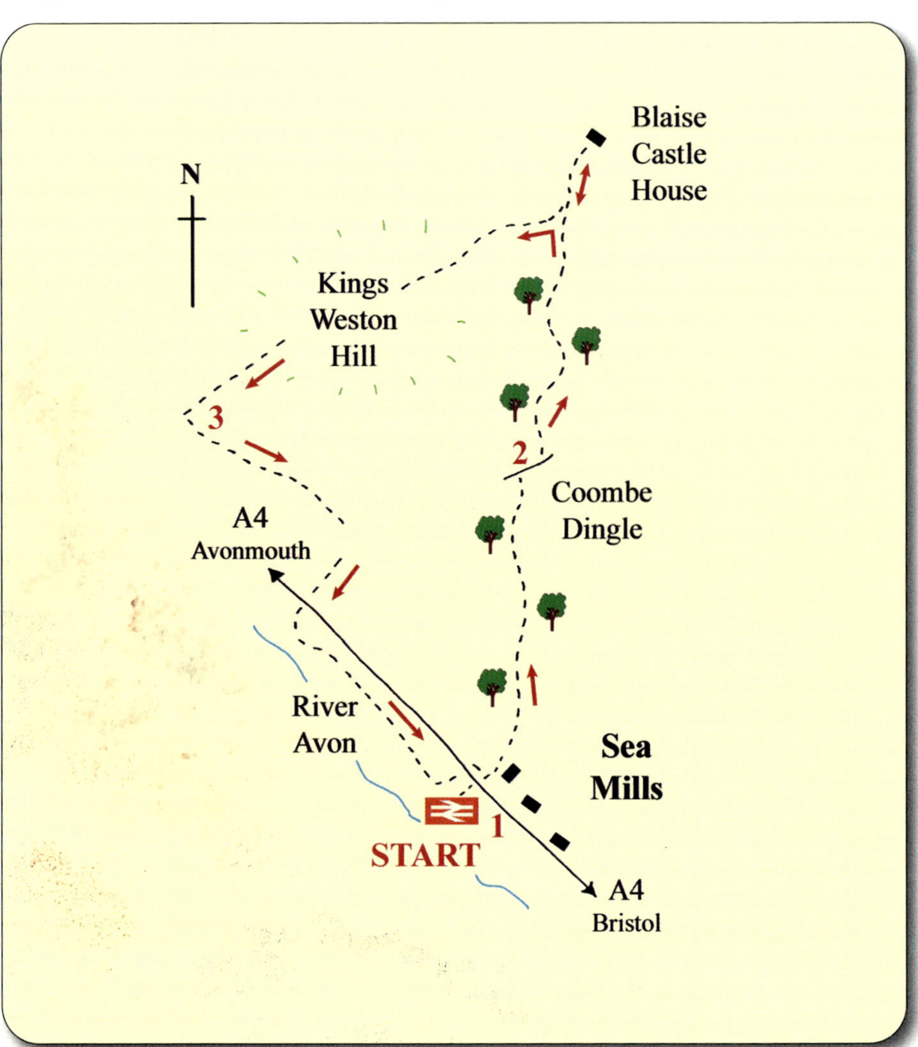

Blaise Castle folly

as it bears right and climbs uphill. In 150 yards, by some black railings on the left, turn sharply left and follow a path climbing up into the woodland. (*Go straight ahead here to reach the open ground surrounding Blaise Castle House*). Ignoring all side turns, follow the main path ahead for 200 yards to reach the second of two viewpoints. Bear right up some steps into an open clearing and **Blaise Castle**. Turn left on reaching the clearing to follow a path alongside a bench that drops downhill to reach an open grassy area, ignoring any side turns. Head across the left edge of this grassland, passing a bench, before following a path into the woodland opposite. In a few paces, veer right at a junction and walk ahead to a major junction of paths. Follow the path ahead – not the broad ride on the right – that climbs the hillside, reaching some steps in 25 yards. On the hilltop, enter an open area of grassland and walk across the hilltop for just over ½ mile to reach an aerial mast on the left. Keep following the path in the same direction, ignoring a path running parallel on the left, to some black gates and an information board.

■ *The river Trym* ■

3 Drop down to a footbridge, cross **Kings Weston Lane** and, in 15 yards, follow a path on the left down to **Shirehampton Road**. Pass through a hand gate opposite to enter the National Trust's **Shirehampton Park**. Walk down the left edge of a golf course and, in the bottom left-hand corner, turn right to follow the bottom edge of the golf course. In 125 yards, pass through a hand gate on the left to join a road – **Sylvan Way**. Turn right and walk down to the **Portway**. Cross this main road, pass through a hand gate opposite and follow a path down through some woodland. In 100 yards, turn left along the Severn Way Bristol Link and follow it down under a railway bridge and through a gateway out into an area of overgrown grassland bordering the river. Turn left – there is no obvious path – and follow this area of grassland for ½ mile to an inlet at **Sea Mills**. Turn left, pass under the railway and road bridges ahead, turn right to cross the **Trym** and reach a road. Follow this road to the right, back to **Sea Mills station**.

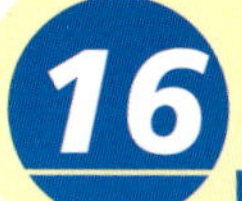

16 Castle Combe and the By Brook Valley

FOOTPATHS FOR FITNESS

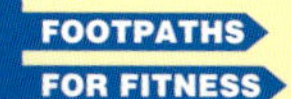

A Variety of Habitats

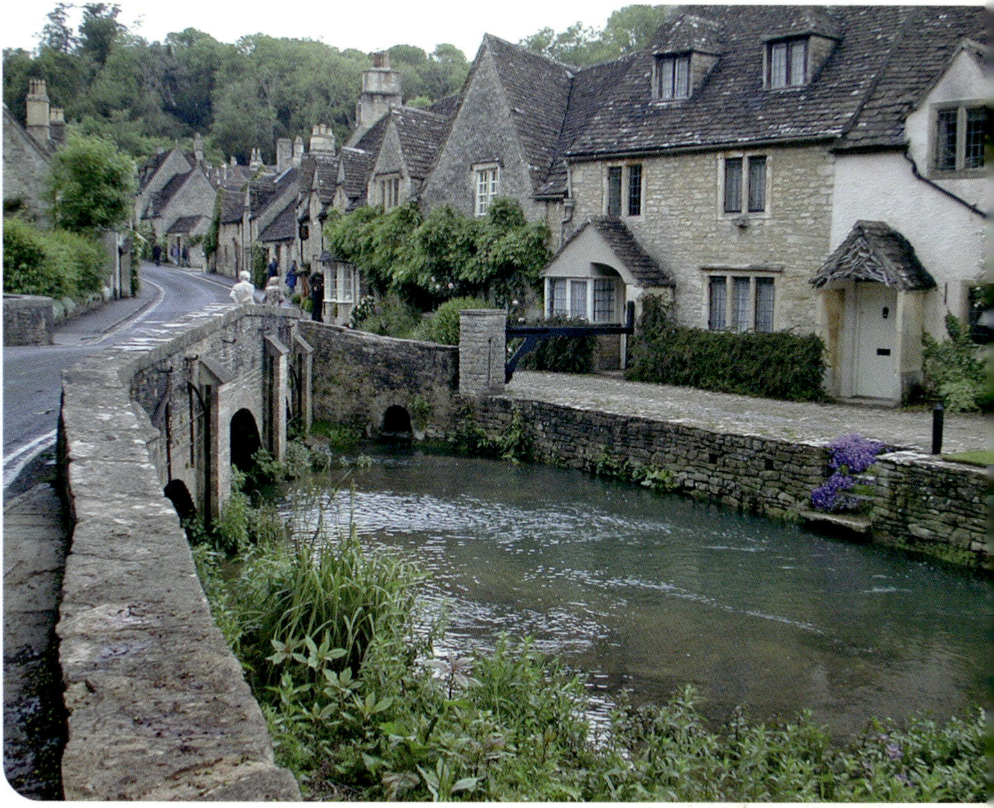

■ *A chocolate box view of Castle Combe* ■

The By Brook is arguably the most attractive of the Bristol Avon's tributaries. Flowing from deep in the southern Cotswolds, it passes through steep wooded valleys close to Castle Combe and Ford, Slaughterford and Box, before joining the Avon at Bathford. The rich array of habitats in the valley – woodland and wetland, water meadows and limestone grassland – are home to an equally rich array of flora and fauna, including buzzards and kestrel, hare and badger, butterfly and orchids. Castle Combe, one of England's most attractive villages, will no doubt engender a sense of déjà vu. The view up through the main street from the

GRADE: 2
ESTIMATED CALORIE BURN: 500

Distance: 4¾ miles
Stiles: 2
Terrain: This walk crosses a generally undulating landscape. There is one climb out of Long Dean on a potentially muddy path, as well as a second climb from Castle Combe back to the car park.
Time: 3 hours
Map: OS Explorer 156
Starting point: GR 845777
Directions to Start / Parking / Public Transport: The visitors' car park for Castle Combe lies in Upper Castle Combe, just off of the B4039 midway between Acton Turville and Chippenham. Castle Combe is not served by a regular public transport service.
Refreshments: Almost at journey's end in Castle Combe, the Castle Inn serves morning coffee and afternoon tea.

packhorse bridge that crosses the By Brook has launched any number of calendars, greetings cards and chocolate boxes! This walk encompasses all of these elements and much more besides – the perfect counter argument to those who believe the Cotswolds only exist north of Cirencester.

1 Leave the car park, turn left and walk up to the B4039. Turn left for 25 yards, before taking the right turn to Grittleton. At a crossroads in 600 yards, turn right along a byway. Follow this byway for ½ mile to its junction with an unclassified road and keep walking ahead for 50 yards to a right-hand bend. At this point, keep ahead along an access road leading to **Summer Lane Cottage**. Beyond this cottage, continue along a track for 600 yards to reach the B4039. Follow this road ahead for 300 yards to a hand gate on the right and a waymarked bridleway.

The White Hart inn near the end of the walk

2 Follow the bridleway across a small pasture to join a drive leading to a cottage. Beyond this property, continue along a track for 75 yards to a pair of gateways. Pass through the left-hand gateway, and follow the field path ahead down through a shallow valley. On reaching a gateway, continue along a track to the next gateway before continuing through the semi-wooded valley bottom to reach a junction in a clearing. Walk across to a gate in the far-right corner of this clearing before continuing along a woodland path to reach the next hand gate. Beyond this gate, follow the

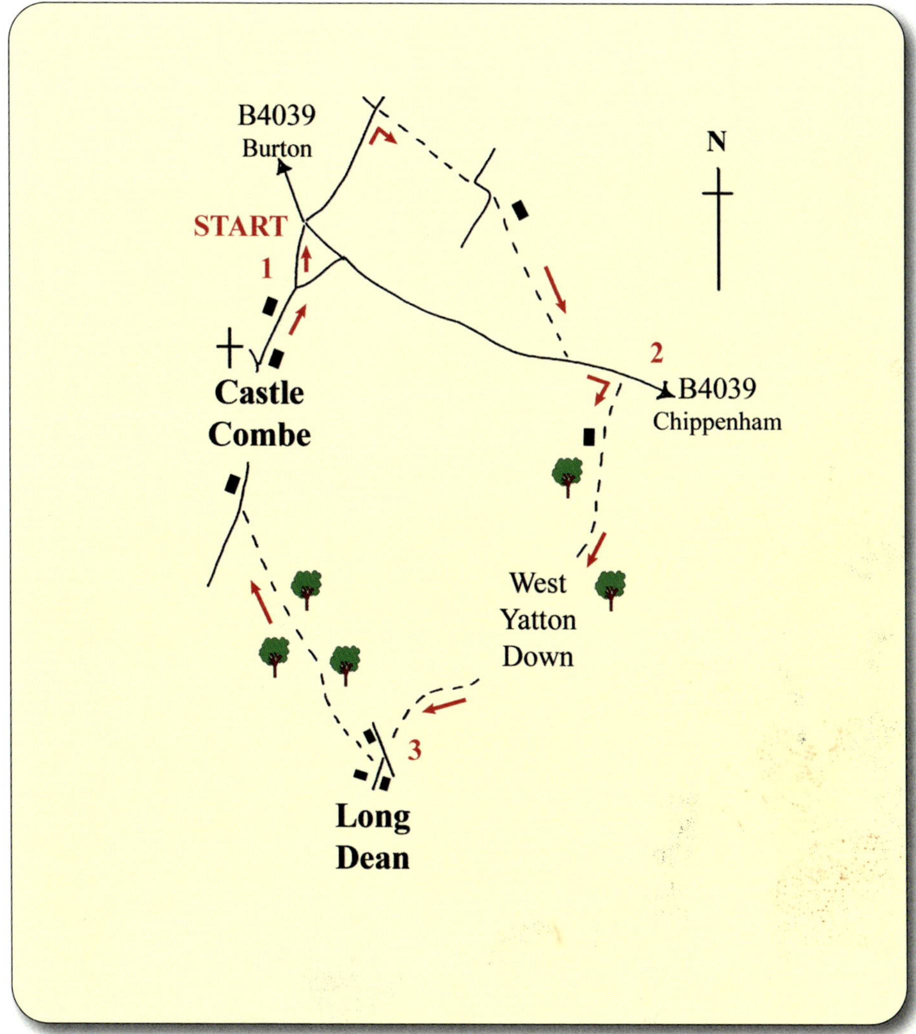

■ *The By Brook flows through a rich variety of habitats* ■

path ahead along the right-hand side of **West Yatton Down**, a dry limestone valley. On the far side of this reserve, keep on the path as it bears left to reach a gate and lane. Follow this lane to the left to a fork, and turn right into **Long Dean**.

3 At a junction in the centre of this hamlet by a letterbox, take a turning on the right which becomes a track leading back to **Castle Combe**. Follow the track uphill out of **Long Dean** to a gate on the hilltop, before continuing ahead to a second gate just 25 yards ahead. Continue following the hilltop path high above the **By Brook** through woodland until the path emerges onto more open hillside in ½ mile. Keep ahead, following the left-hand field boundary, to a stile in the far-left corner of the field by **By Brook**. Continue along the path by the river, before crossing a bridge to join the **Ford** to **Castle Combe** road. Turn right, and follow the road up through the main street in **Castle Combe** to the market place. Follow the road to the right of the market cross for 350 yards to a left turn that leads back to the car park.

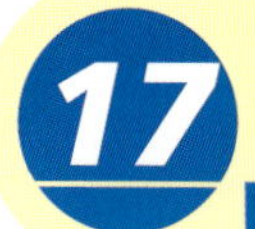

17 Marshfield and the Cotswold Plateau

FOOTPATHS FOR FITNESS

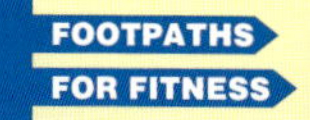

High Hills and Green Lanes

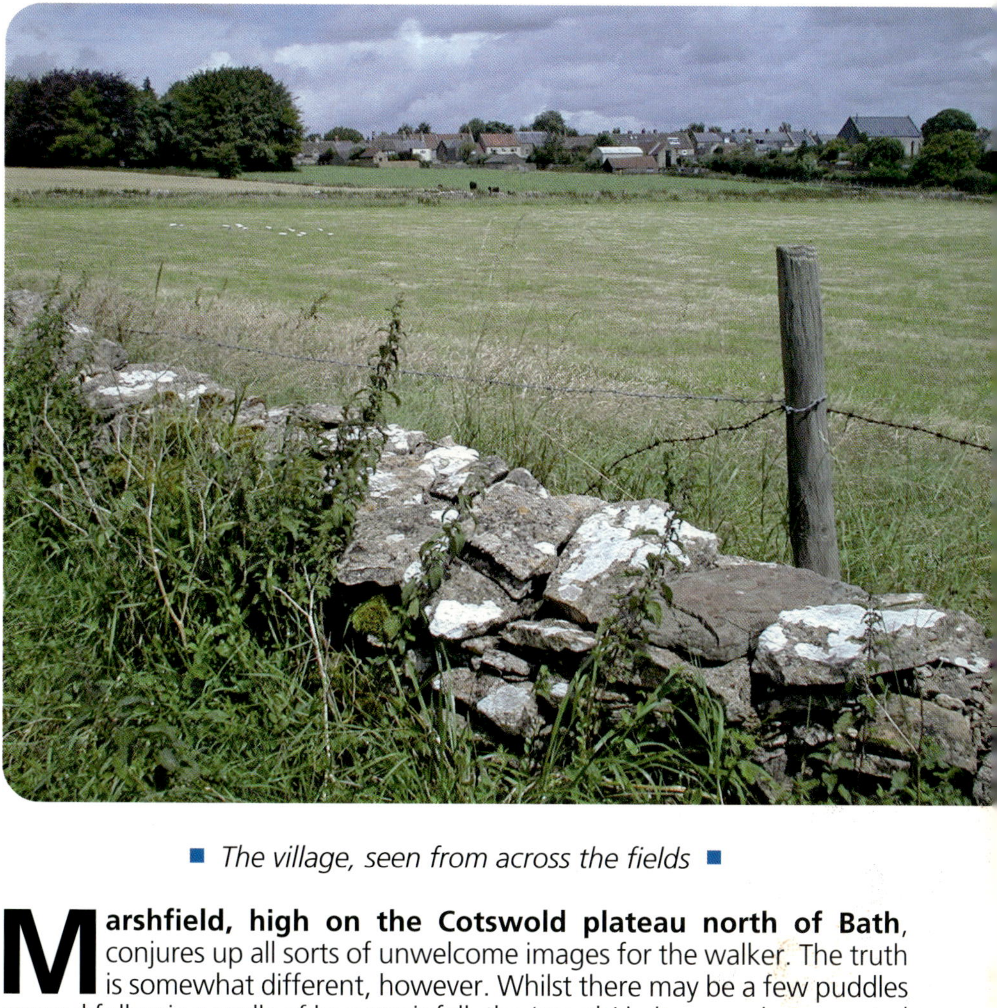

■ *The village, seen from across the fields* ■

Marshfield, high on the Cotswold plateau north of Bath, conjures up all sorts of unwelcome images for the walker. The truth is somewhat different, however. Whilst there may be a few puddles around following spells of heavy rainfall, the 'marsh' in its name is connected with the Old English 'mearc' which translates to a boundary – as in the Welsh Marches. So what we have here is quite literally a settlement that grew up around a border field, but quite what the border was is now lost in the sands of time. Marshfield is very much a border settlement in another sense, too. The village stands at the divide of two very distinct landscapes.

GRADE: 2
ESTIMATED CALORIE BURN: 500

Distance: 5 miles
Stiles: 4
Terrain: A landscape typified by gentle undulations rather then steep hills. This makes for a relatively easy walk – although it is quite high on miles.
Time: 3 hours
Map: OS Explorer 155
Starting point: GR 773738
Directions to Start / Parking / Public Transport: From the junction of the A420 with the A46 at Cold Ashton, north of Bath, follow the A420 towards Chippenham for 2 miles before turning right into Marshfield. Park somewhere in the vicinity of the almshouses that lie on the left-hand side of the High Street as you enter the village. Marshfield is served by an occasional bus service from Chippenham.
Refreshments: Sweetapples Tea Shop is in the centre of Marshfield. When this is closed on Sundays, there is a selection of nearby pubs.

To the north lie the gentle undulations of the Cotswold plateau, flat looking fields bordered by dry stone walls. To the south, the view and the country is quite different, for there one is quickly into the wooded valleys and hedge-lined fields that are so typical of this corner of north-east Somerset. It is this delightful pastoral landscape that forms the focus of the walk. There are few man-made features to catch the eye – rather it is open views and peaceful green lanes, a place that is far from the proverbial madding crowd.

Attractive almshouses in Marshfield

1 Walk the length of the **High Street** and, at its eastern end, by a war memorial, bear right into **Market Place**. Follow **Market Place** around to **Little End**, and continue ahead along this cul de sac.

Having followed this lane around a left-hand bend, turn immediately right down an enclosed footpath to a stile. Cross the stile and follow the left edge of the field ahead down to a stile. Cross this stile and bear half-left and climb to a stile in the top corner of the field.

2 Walk ahead across the next field to a hand gate, before walking straight ahead across the next field – passing to the right of a telegraph pole – to a hand gate on the far side of the field. Walk uphill in the next field, a field

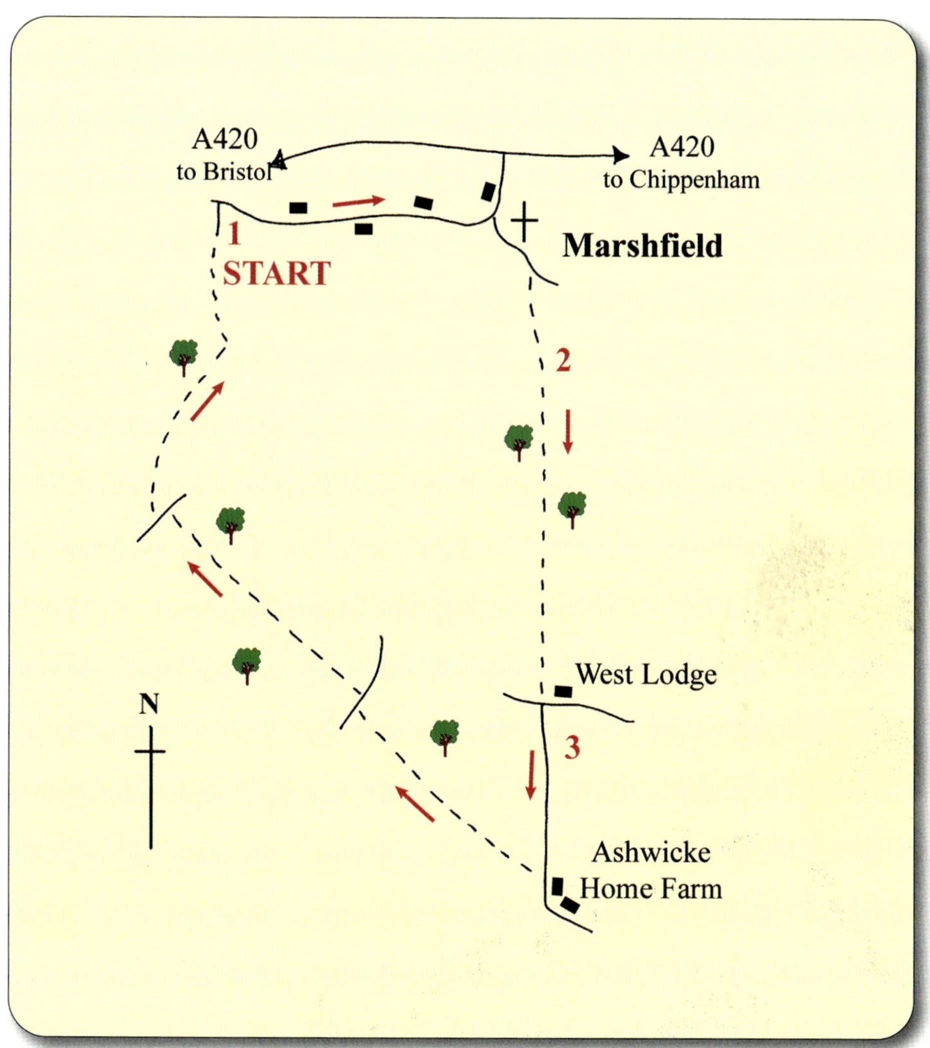

■ *A quiet footpath* ■

boundary on the left and, where this boundary ends, keep walking directly ahead to a stile in the corner of the field. Beyond this stile, follow the right edge of the next field down to a gap in the hedgerow at the bottom of the field. Walk ahead across the middle of the next field to a hand gate opposite, follow the left edge of the next field to a hand gate, cross a drive to a gate opposite and follow the left edge of the next field down to a lane.

3 Follow the lane ahead for 350 yards and, immediately before the buildings of **Ashwicke Home Farm**, turn right through a gateway and follow the left edge of a field across to its left-hand corner. Join an enclosed path and continue for ¼ mile to join **Ayford Lane**. Turn right along this lane and, in 100 yards, left onto a bridleway. Follow this track for ¾ mile to **Beek's Lane**. Turn left and, in 50 yards, turn right onto a bridleway. Follow this track for ¾ mile through to its junction with the **High Street** in **Marshfield**, before turning right to return to your vehicle.

18 Around the Badminton Estate

FOOTPATHS FOR FITNESS

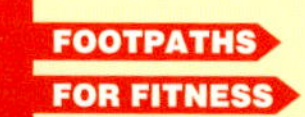

A Charming Pastoral Landscape

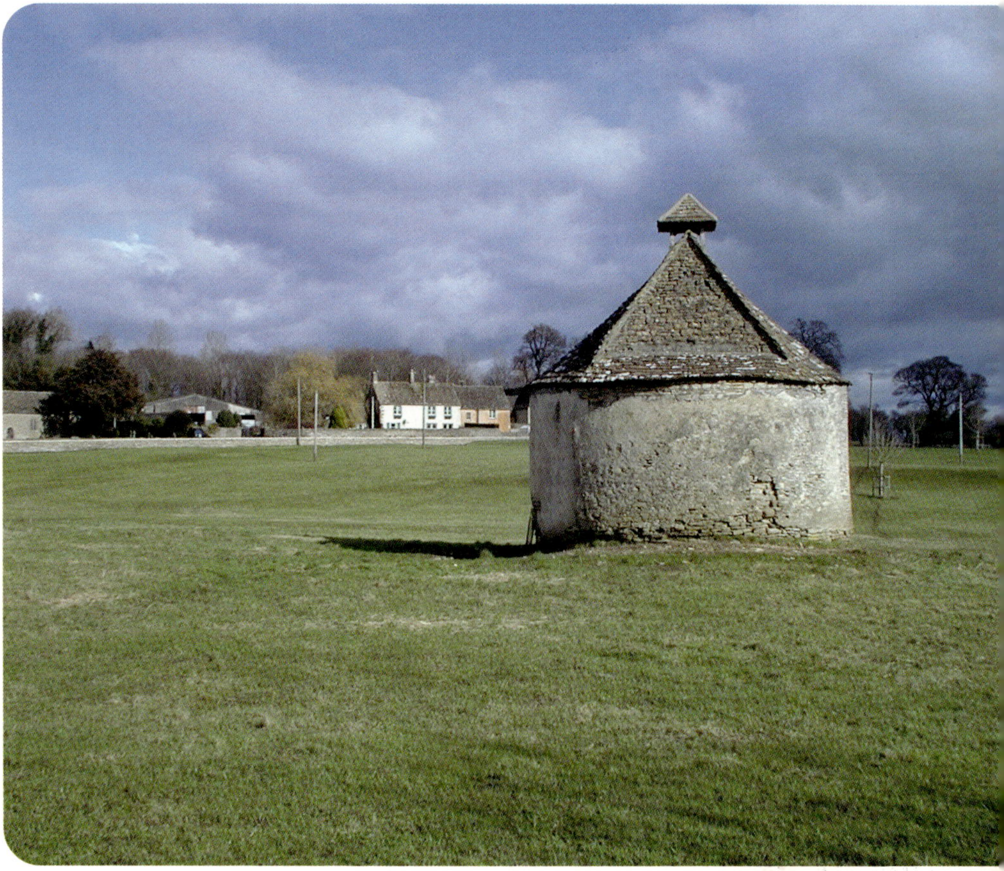

A dovecote in Little Badminton

Great Badminton and Little Badminton, Sopworth and Luckington – a quartet of delightful Cotswold-style villages scattered in and around the Badminton Estate. The landscape may be gently undulating rather than spectacular, but it is the human interest that makes this such a charming corner of the country. Here can be found traditional stone cottages and ancient churches, drystone walls and fine old inns, grand mansions and secluded country lanes. Naturally, there are horses everywhere

– Badminton is, of course, the focus for one of the world's premier three-day events – with the consequent stables, paddocks and jumps dotted around the landscape. Above everything else, it is a charming pastoral landscape, the perfect setting for one of the final – and more challenging – walks in this book.

1 Walk back down to the end of the **High Street**, and follow the private road opposite – it is a public footpath – up past various estate buildings to some gates by a lodge. Walk ahead across the deer park, keeping left at a fork by an oak tree, and continue to a hand gate by a lodge on the far side of the park. Follow a lane around to the right, through **Little Badminton**, passing the church, to a junction with the main road. Turn right and follow the road for 400 yards to **Shepherd's Lodge**. Turn right and follow the road down to a left-hand bend. Continue following the road as it runs through an avenue of trees across to a junction in 1 mile. Turn right, and follow the road through woodland to a junction in 500 yards by cottages.

2 Continue along the lane ahead for 400 yards to a bridleway on the left. Follow this track up to an old gateway and continue along a grassy ride to the far side of a field. Continue on the bridleway through woodland and

GRADE: 3
ESTIMATED CALORIE BURN: 750

Distance: 7½ miles
Stiles: 2
Terrain: A landscape typified by gentle undulations, rather then steep hills. This makes for a relatively easy walk – although it is quite high on miles.
Time: 4 hours
Map: OS Explorer 168
Starting point: GR 805826
Directions to Start / Parking / Public Transport: Follow an unclassified road from the B4039 at Acton Turville into Great Badminton and, on a sharp left-hand bend, turn right into the High Street. At the end of the High Street, turn right into Haye's Lane and park outside the memorial hall. Badminton is not served by a regular public transport service.
Refreshments: The Old Royal Ship Inn at Luckington will provide welcome refreshments well over halfway around the route.

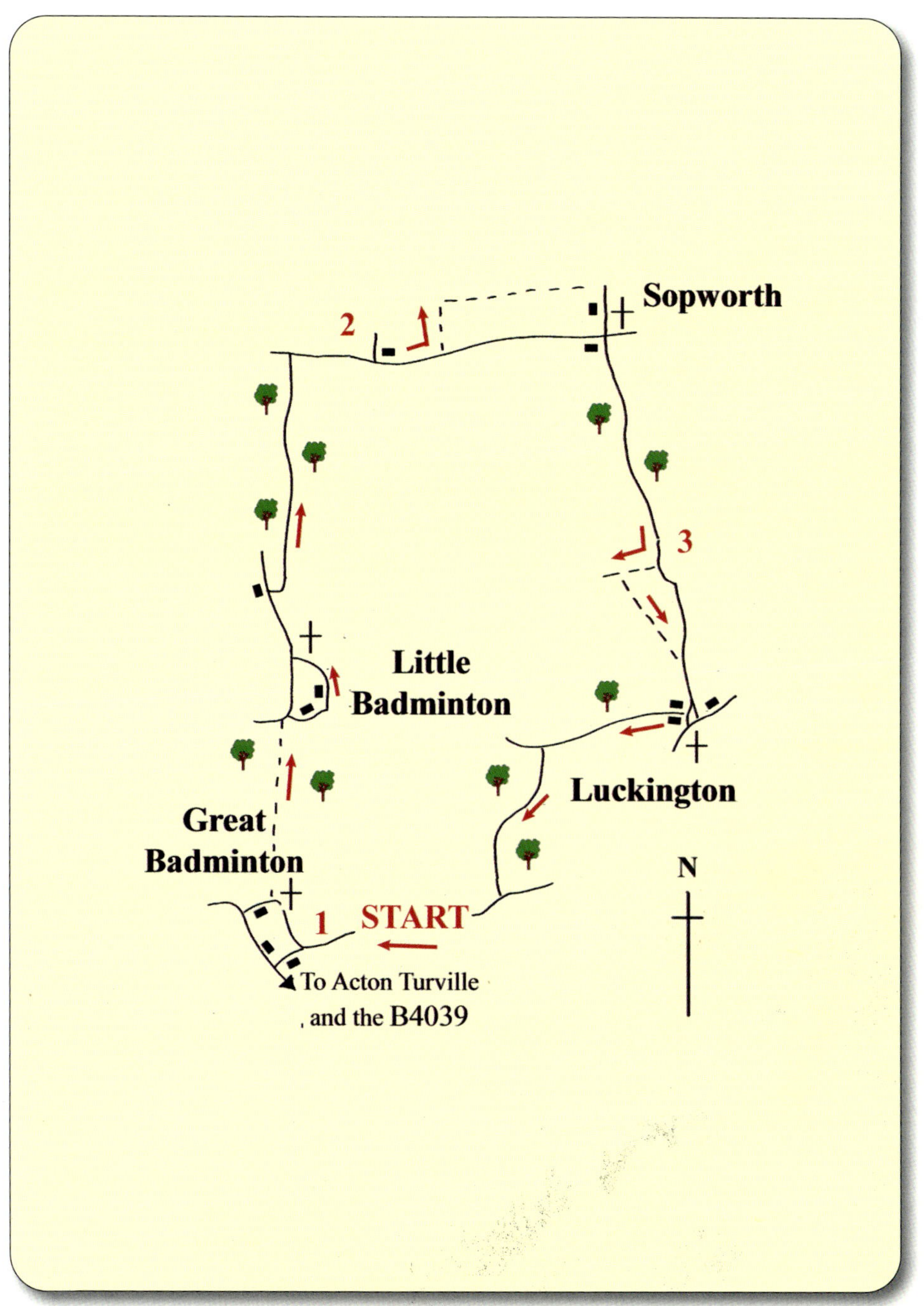
Sopworth
2
3
Little
Badminton
Luckington
Great
Badminton
N
1
START
To Acton Turville
and the B4039

through a gateway into an open field. Follow the right edge of this field for 100 yards, turn right and follow what is known as the **Wiltshire Path** for ¾ mile to a lane in **Sopworth** by **Wiltshire Path Cottage**. Turn right into the village and, in 150 yards, left along **Church Lane** to the church. Turn right at the end of **Church Lane** down an enclosed footpath to rejoin the road in **Sopworth**. Follow the road ahead out of **Sopworth** to a crossroads, and continue ahead towards **Luckington**. In ½ mile, ignore a cul de sac lane on the right, and keep ahead for 100 yards to a track on the right.

3 Turn right and, in 100 yards, cross a stile in the hedgerow on the left. Walk down to the bottom left corner of the field ahead, pass through a gap in the hedgerow and head across the next field – bearing left all the while – to a stile opposite. Cross to the far-left corner of the following field, making for a small stable block, and pass through a hand gate before joining a lane. Follow the lane to the right into **Luckington**, keeping ahead at all junctions, to reach the B4040 by the village green. Turn right and, by the village store, turn right into **The Street** and walk up to a junction. Take the left turn

Sopworth, a delightful Cotswold-style village

■ *A quiet country lane* ■

waymarked to **Cherry Orchard**. In 300 yards, keep left at a junction – the cul de sac lane ahead goes to **Cherry Orchard** – and follow a very quiet lane for ¾ mile to a junction, passing **Allengrove Farm** along the way. Turn right and follow **Luckington Lane** for ¾ mile into **Great Badminton**. Turn right into **Haye's Lane** to return to the memorial hall.

Littleton, Oldbury and the Severn Estuary

A Walk for All Seasons

Oldbury Pill with boats waiting for the tide

Littleton-upon- Severn and Oldbury-on-Severn both now lie some way inland from the great river itself. In centuries past, however, the waters of this mighty estuary would have come right up to these villages, with the local meadows being damp, low-lying marshland. Flood defence systems have given the local residents a much safer and drier existence! This walk follows a series of undulating field paths and tracks between Littleton and Oldbury – with their slight elevation giving tantalising glimpses of the Severn – before a magnificent stroll along the riverbank. At high tide, the river's treacherous currents are plain to see, whilst at low tide thousands of waders will be seen feasting on the mudflats. The views are expansive and far-ranging. Close at hand is the river with the two Severn crossings, whilst across the water lies the Forest of Dean and the distant Welsh hills. Along the way, St Arilda's church will prove a real gem, sitting atop a diminutive knoll and with a churchyard seat that commands the most delightful of views. This is a route for all seasons, but is especially worth walking in the winter months when flocks of migratory birds make the river their home.

1 Walk back along the road towards Elberton for 150 yards to a stile in the hedge on the left. Cross this stile and follow a path called the **Jubilee Way** across the left edges of 2 fields to a piece of wooden fencing. Cross the fence, cross a stile on the left and bear half-right in the next field to a stile in the middle of the right-hand field boundary. Cross a lane to a stile opposite, before heading up the right-hand side of the hillside field ahead to a wooden barrier on the right in the top corner of the field. Cross this

GRADE: 3
ESTIMATED CALORIE BURN: 700

Distance: 6½ miles
Stiles: 12
Terrain: Other than one relatively steep climb out of Littleton-upon-Severn at the start of the walk, the route follows level and easily walked paths. It is necessary to climb over a pair of gates to cross Oldbury Pill. There are also a good number of stiles on this walk, which is clearly one of the more demanding in the book.
Time: 4 hours
Map: OS Explorer 167
Starting point: GR 595899
Directions to Start / Parking / Public Transport: Leave the M48 at junction 1 and follow the B4461 for 2 miles into Elberton. Turn left in the village to follow an unclassified road to Littleton-upon-Severn. After 1 mile, on the right-hand bend at the entrance to the village, park on the left in front of the village hall. Littleton is not served by a regular public transport service.
Refreshments: The Anchor Inn at Oldbury will provide refreshment en route, whilst the White Hart at Littleton – 200 yards down the main street from the village hall – will prove an excellent diversion at journey's end.

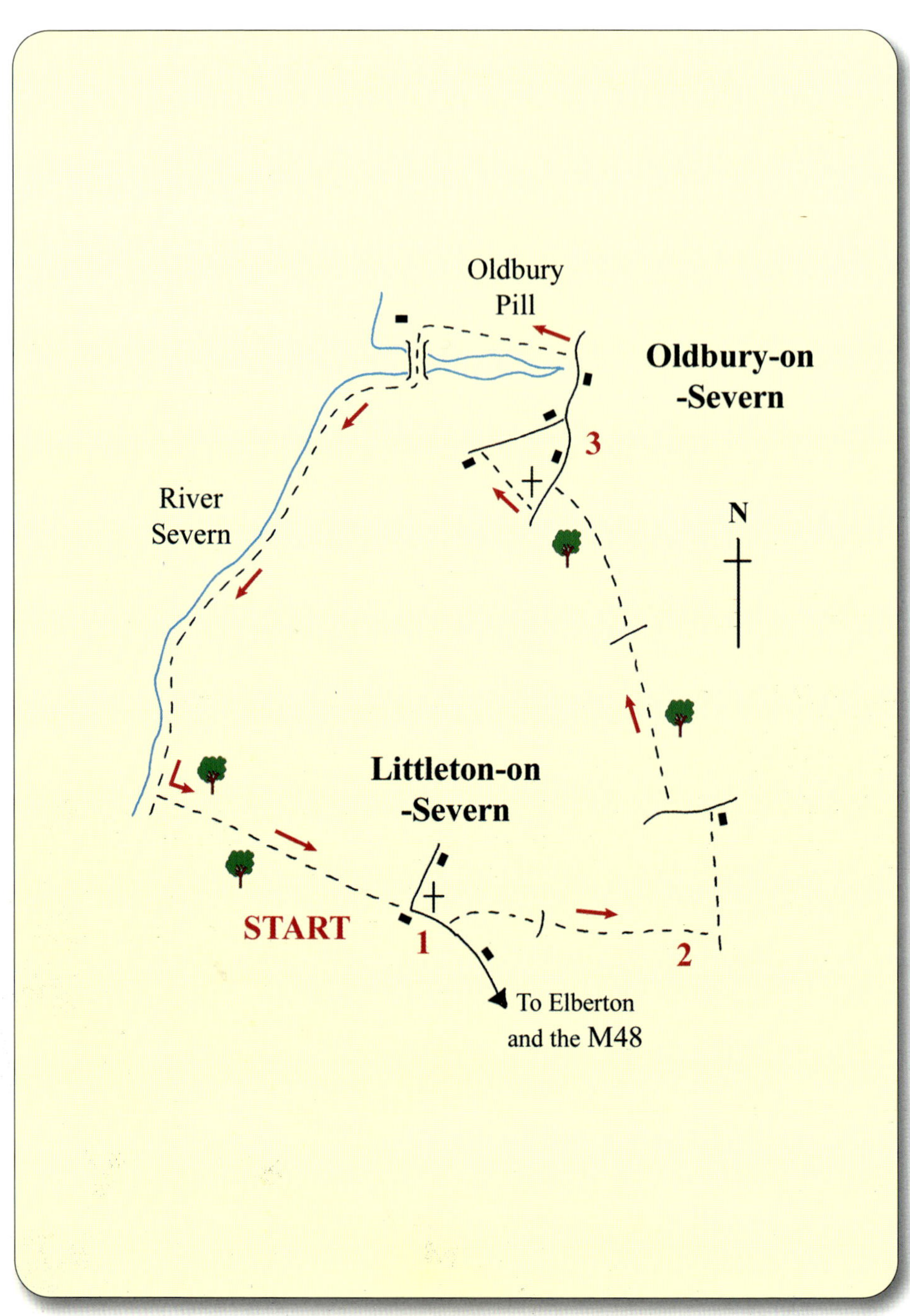
Oldbury
Pill
Oldbury-on
-Severn
3
River
Severn
N
Littleton-on
-Severn
START
1
2
To Elberton
and the M48

■ *St Arilda's church, a real gem* ■

barrier, walk ahead for a few paces and turn left to a stile. Follow the right-hand edge of the next field around to a stile in its far right-hand corner. Cross this stile, walk ahead for a few paces to a track and bear left to a hand gate. Beyond this gate, head uphill in the next field to a gate in the top field boundary. Follow the right edge of the field ahead – woodland on the right – and where the woodland ends, keep ahead across the field following a rough track. On the far side of the field, just to the left of the track, cross a pair of stiles in the hedgerow.

2 Beyond these stiles, walk across the field ahead to a hand gate in the left-hand field boundary 100 yards up from the corner of the field. Join a track – Bond Lane – turn left and follow the track for ½ mile to an unclassified road. Turn left and then, in 300 yards, right onto a bridleway immediately past a telegraph pole. Follow this track, which becomes a wide grassy ride at one point, for ½ mile to a lane. Cross the lane and follow the track opposite to a junction in ¼ mile. Keep walking ahead along a track that joins a lane in 250 yards. Turn left, and follow the road along to **St Arilda's church**. Enter the churchyard, walk around to the far side of the church

■ *Enjoying the view across the Severn* ■

and drop down some steps to a gate at the exit of the churchyard. Continue along a dozen more steps, and turn right to a hand gate in the hedgerow. Walk across the field ahead to a stile in the opposite hedgerow, 50 yards down from the corner of the field. Follow the left edge of the following field down to a lane in its bottom left-hand corner. Follow the lane to the right for 300 yards to the main road in **Oldbury-on-Severn**.

3 Turn left, pass the Anchor Inn, cross **Oldbury Pill** and turn left along the drive leading to the local sailing club. In 200 yards, veer left and follow a grassy path that runs alongside the **Pill** to reach a track by a sluice gate. Cross the sluice gate and follow the raised grassy embankment – a flood defence – towards the **Severn Bridge**. In 1¼ miles, pass around a muddy inlet – **Whale Wharf** – and continue following the raised embankment towards **Severn Bridge** for ¼ mile. Drop down the embankment on the left to a hand gate and a footpath. Follow the left edge of the field ahead to a track in the left-hand corner, before continuing along the track ahead to a gate. Continue along the track to the right – and very shortly to the left – before continuing for just under ¾ mile to the road in **Littleton-upon-Severn**. Turn right back to the village hall.

20 Monkton Combe, Midford and Combe Hay

FOOTPATHS FOR FITNESS

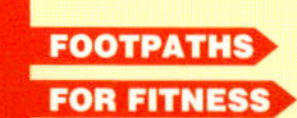

Interest at Every Turn

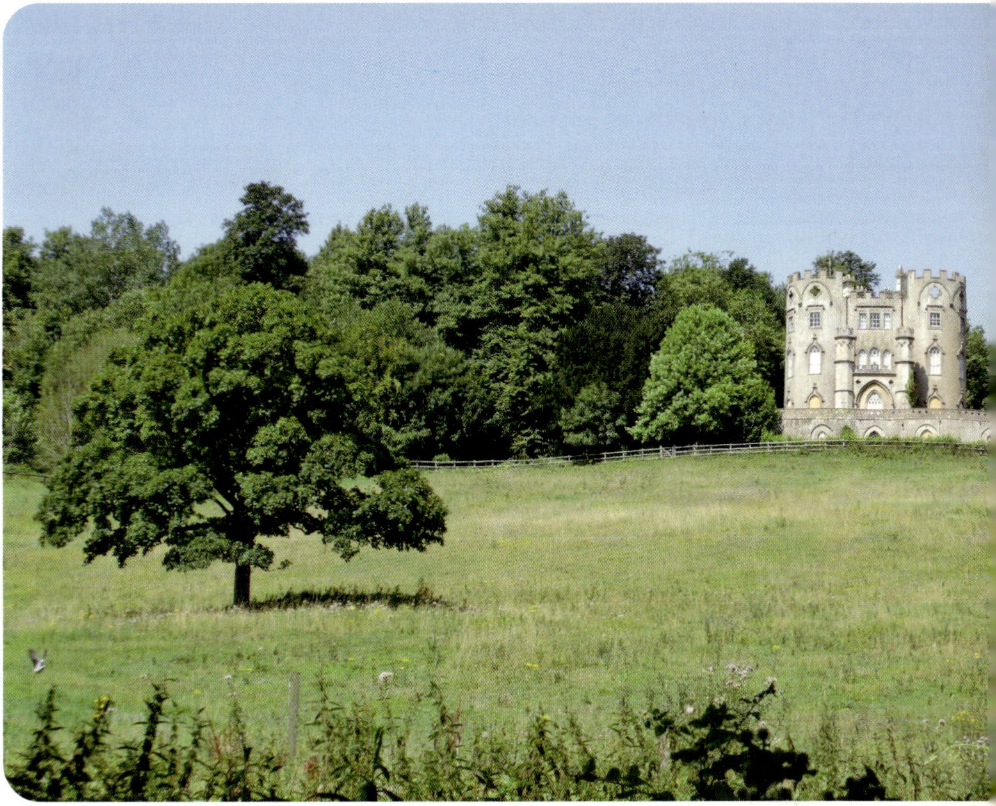

■ *The walk passes close to the privately-owned Midford Castle* ■

Head south from Bath and very soon there is a delightful landscape of rolling hills and deep valleys. A series of diminutive rivers water the valley bottoms – Wellow Brook, Cam Brook and Midford Brook in this case - with human interest at every turn. The walk starts out from Monkton Combe – with its Victorian public school and church – and heads out as far as Combe Hay – where every property will have you breaking that tenth commandment that relates to not coveting thy neighbour's house! Along the way is the hamlet of Tucking Mill – with its secretive reservoir and a property that was once home to William Smith, the father of geology – as well as Midford – where the industrial archaeologist will be drooling at the collection of railway viaducts, a canal aqueduct and lock chambers. The canal in question is the Somerset Coal Canal, whose extensive remains dominate the latter stages of the walk. Should this talk of railways and canals suggest a grim landscape, have no fears. It is the outstanding natural landscape that is the main feature of this walk – open views, ancient woodland, valley bottoms and sparkling streams.

1 Walk through the churchyard to a hand gate in the end boundary wall, join a lane and turn left. In 600 yards, immediately past **Tucking Mill Cottage**, turn right and follow a footpath up to Tucking Mill Reservoir. Keep ahead along the reservoir access road and, immediately before a railway viaduct, climb some steps on the left to reach the former railway track bed. Turn left, and follow the trackbed for ½ mile into the car park of the Hope & Anchor at **Midford**. Continue following the trackbed – crossing a viaduct – and continue for 100 yards to an exit point from the railway path on the

GRADE: 3
ESTIMATED CALORIE BURN: 700

Distance: 7 miles
Stiles: 4
Terrain: Although this is a generally level walk, there is one hard climb from Midford uphill into Twinhoe. This is followed by a compensatory descent into Combe Hay.
Time: 4 hours
Map: OS Explorers 142 and 155
Starting point: GR 772620
Directions to Start / Parking / Public Transport: Follow the A36 south from Bath to its junction with the B3108 Bradford-on-Avon road. Just before the traffic lights, turn right and head up Brassknocker Hill. In 100 yards, turn left along the lane leading to Monkton Combe village. Park on the roadside between the Wheelwrights Arms and the church. *First* run regular buses from Bath to Trowbridge that stop on the A36 at the foot of Brassknocker Hill.
Refreshments: There are a number of inns on this route – the Wheelwrights Arms at Monkton Combe, the Hope and Anchor at Midford and the Wheatsheaf at Combe Hay. These are all gastro pubs – so the food is not cheap – but a decent meal could be your reward for completing this collection of walks!

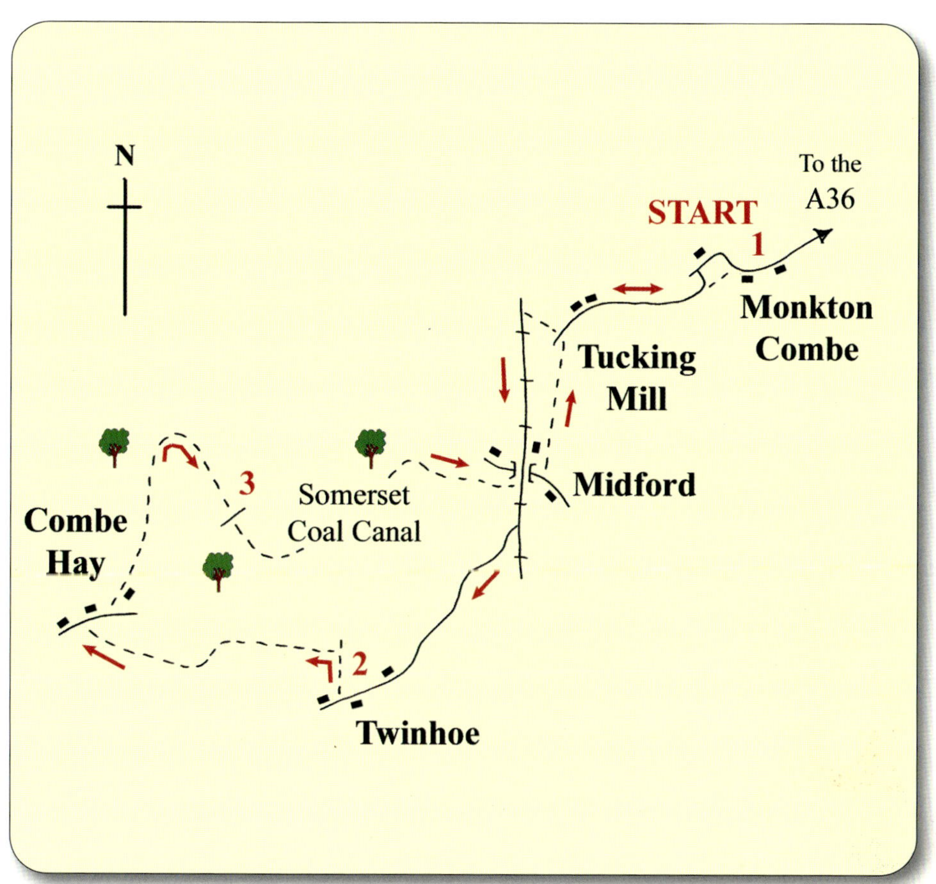

right. Leave the railway path, and turn left along a lane. Follow this lane uphill and across the hilltop for 1 mile to a junction by **Middle Twinhoe Farm**. Follow the road ahead for 200 yards to a bridleway on the right, just before Upper Twinhoe Farm.

2 Turn right, and follow the track downhill for 100 yards before turning left through a hand gate to join a bridleway. Follow this path around the left edge of an arable field to its far corner, before turning right to follow the path around **Brake Wood** to reach a hand gate. Continue following a field path – it becomes a track that passes through woodland – dropping steadily downhill to reach a farm gate and open field. Follow the right edge of this field and continue following what becomes a track down to a gate. Continue along the track down to the road in **Combe Hay**. Turn right,

passing the **Wheatsheaf Inn**, and in 150 yards turn left along a no through road. Follow this road up to and past a series of properties on the right. Beyond the last property, continue along a track for 200 yards – passing **Rowley Farm Stables** – to a gate. Cross a stile on the right, and follow the right edge of the field ahead downhill and into a belt of trees. Just inside the woodland, cross a stile on the left and follow a path along to a ruinous building. Veer right, and drop downhill through beech woodland to a footbridge over a stream. Walk ahead a few paces to a stile, turn right and follow a path bordering the **Somerset Coal Canal** for 250 yards to a stile and lane opposite **Bridge Farm**.

3 Pass through a hand gate opposite – slightly to the left – and continue along a footpath running alongside a paddock to reach a hand gate and junction of paths. Turn right for a few paces, before turning left through a hand gate to enter a meadow. Walk the length of this meadow, passing through one gate along way, to reach a hand gate in ½ mile just before a railway embankment. Beyond this gate, follow a path to the right under a viaduct,

■ *Midford Brook in reflective mood* ■

■ *Tucking Mill Cottage passed along the way* ■

and then to the left around to another gate. Follow the path ahead across a field, the bed of the coal canal on the left, to a gate on the far side of the field in some trees. Continue along an enclosed path to reach the B3110 by the **Hope & Anchor** in **Midford**. Turn right and, in a short distance, just past a property on the left called the **Moorings**, turn left along a public footpath. In 50 yards, keep on the path as it veers left up a bank to follow a fence into an area of woodland. Follow the woodland path – the bed of the coal canal on the left – for ½ mile to the road by **Tucking Mill Cottage**. Follow this road to the right for 600 yards to a left-hand bend on the edge of **Monkton Combe**. On this bend, pass through a hand gate on the right and follow a path back through the churchyard to the road in the centre of **Monkton Combe**.

Calorie Chart

The following chart shows the approximate calories spent per hour by a person weighing 8 stone (112 lbs), 11 stone (154 lbs) and 15 stone (210 lbs)

	8 stone	11 stone	15 stone
Walking, 2 mph	160	240	312
Walking, 3 mph	210	320	416
Walking, 4½ mph	295	440	572

Note that these figures are based on moderate, not vigorous, activity.